Health Education and Community Pharmacy

Health Education and Community Pharmacy

N. KUMAR
B.Sc., M.Sc., Ph.D., PGDCA, PGDPM
Bangalore University, Karnataka

AITBS PUBLISHERS, INDIA
MEDICAL PUBLISHERS
J-5/6, Krishan Nagar, Delhi-110051 (INDIA)
Phone: 011-40167052, 49067602
E-mail: aitbsindia@gmail.com & aitbsindia@hotmail.com

First Edition : 2009
Second Edition : 2026

ISBN: 978-81-7473-438-9

Published by:
Virender Kumar Arya for
AITBS Publishers, India
Medical Publishers
J-5/6, Krishan Nagar, Delhi-110051 (INDIA)
Phone: 011-40167052, 49067602
E-mail: aitbsindia@gmail.com & aitbsindia@hotmail.com

Printed by AITBS, Delhi

PREFACE

Health education is a high-profile topic for national government, local authorities, health authorities, and educational agencies. Health Education plays a crucial role in the development of a healthy, inclusive and equitable social, psychological and physical environment. It reflects current best practice, using an empowering, multi-dimensional, multi-professional approach which relates to all settings, organizations, and parts and levels of society, including schools, colleges, universities, the health services, the community and the workplace.

The various journals and scholars reflects the best of modern thinking about health education, offers stimulating and incisive coverage of current debates, concerns, interventions, and initiatives, and provides a wealth of evidence, research, information, and ideas to inform and inspire those in both the theory and practice of health education.

On the other hand, unfortunately Pharmacy practices in India has not been recognized as an integral part of the emerging pharmaceutical challenges and the attention it requires to prepare them to play their role as resourceful Community Pharmacists. The necessity to improve the pharmacy practices on professional scales cannot be ignored nor delayed in the context of emerging changes, when India is becoming a fast developing nation in the world.

This calls for innovative marketing dynamics in every industrial activity. In pharmaceuticals as a healthcare industry, India has already proved its technical competence and capabilities by producing basic drugs and formulations, in every therapeutic segment including preventive medicines for both domestic and global markets.

In this context it is crucial that we take bold initiative to educate the practicing pharmacists, change their mind set and prepare them as Community Pharmacists by introducing refresher courses at State and District Headquarters with a time frame.

A large work is difficult because it is large, even though all its parts might singly be performed with facility; where there are many things to be done, each must be allowed its share of time and labour, in the proportion only which it bears to the whole; nor can it be expected, that the stones which form the dome of a temple, should be squared and polished like the diamond of a ring.

I extend my sincere and whole-heartly thanks to *Virender Kumar Arya,* the publisher of A.I.T.B.S. Publishers, India for his motivating guidance and cheerful co-operation of his staff members during preparation of this book.

Author

CONTENTS

■■■

1

Introduction to Health Education and Community Pharmacy

HEALTH EDUCATION

Health education is the art of persuading people, with the help of the educational process, to adopt such practices as are good for their health, and give up those that are harmful. It attempts to transform knowledge about disease-prevention and health-promotion into conduct routinely practised by the common people. Communication, information and education are the tools used to bring about such transformation. The three-fold objectives of health education are the following:

- To ensure people adopt healthy life styles and persist with them.
- To help them utilize the available health services wisely.
- To assist them take decisions individually and collectively for achieving positive health.

Significance: Health education is the sole means of prevention in the case of diseases like accidents, AIDS, dental caries and periodontal disease.

In the case of diseases for which preventive measures (The immunizations, protective clothing, etc.) are available, health education plays the role of a catalyst: it drives the persons to accept them and promotes their acceptance by the people. The availability of health services free of cost may or may not lead to their acceptance; but if such services are combined with health education the chances of people accepting them are greatly enhanced. Where a person has to take drugs or use contraceptives for prolonged periods, health education ensures he or she persists with the drug or contraceptive for the prescribed duration. In a community project for the control of hookworm infestation in a rural area, each and every house was provided with a sanitary latrine.

When a survey was done a year later, it was found that there was no decrease at all in the magnitude of the disease. The reason for this was that no one had made use of the latrine; the villagers persisted with attending to the call of nature in the open fields. They did not make use of the latrines, because they were never told about the need and importance of doing so.

TYPES OF HEALTH EDUCATION

There are two kinds of health education: informal and formal.

Informal education: Informal variety is the education of the children by their parents in such matters as washing of hands, urinating or defecating only in the toilet, eating at regular hours, covering mouth while coughing, etc. These health (and other) habits become ingrained into the child's mind and persist life-long.

Formal education: Formal health education is carried out under three different situations:

(i) *Education of patients by their physicians* as part of management, for example, education about salt restriction given by the doctor to a patient suffering from high blood pressure. This kind of education is known as *'bed-side education.'*

(ii) *Education of high-risk individuals* (the so-called 'high-risk strategy'). Examples are the education of the smokers to give up the habit, of the obese to reduce their weight, and of the prostitutes to insist that their customers use Nirodh.

(iii) *Education of the community at large,* for example, education of the mothers about nutrition in pregnancy, education of school children about the dangers of smoking, alcoholism and drugs; and the education of the community about the small family norm.

COMMUNITY PHARMACY

Pharmacy is the health profession that links the health sciences with the chemical sciences, and it is charged with ensuring the safe and effective use of medication. The scope of pharmacy practice includes more traditional roles such as compounding and dispensing medications, and it also includes more modern services related to patient care, including clinical services, reviewing medications for safety and efficacy, and providing drug information. Pharmacists, therefore, are the experts on drug therapy and are the primary health professionals who optimize medication use to provide patients with positive health outcomes. The term is also applied to an establishment used for such purposes.

The field of Pharmacy can generally be divided into three primary disciplines:

- Pharmaceutics
- Medicinal chemistry and Pharmacognosy
- Pharmacy practice

The boundaries between these disciplines and with other sciences, such as biochemistry, are not always clear-cut; and often, collaborative teams from various disciplines research together.

Pharmacology is sometimes considered a fourth discipline of pharmacy. Although pharmacology is essential to the study of pharmacy, it is not specific to pharmacy. Therefore, it is usually considered to be a field of the broader sciences.

Community pharmacies usually consist of a retail storefront with a dispensary where medications are stored and dispensed. The dispensary is subject to pharmacy legislation; with requirements for storage conditions, compulsory texts, equipment, etc., specified in legislation. Where it was once the case that pharmacists stayed within the dispensary compounding/dispensing medications; there has been an increasing trend towards the use of trained pharmacy technicians while the pharmacist spends more time communicating with patients.

All pharmacies are required to have a pharmacist on-duty at all times when open. In many jurisdictions, it is also a requirement that the owner of a pharmacy must be a registered pharmacist (R.Ph.). This latter requirement has been revoked in many jurisdictions, such that many retailers (including supermarkets and mass merchandisers) now include a pharmacy as a department of their store.

Likewise, many pharmacies are now rather grocery store-like in their design. In addition to medicines and prescriptions, many now sell a diverse arrangement of additional household items such as cosmetics, shampoo, office supplies, confectionary, and snack foods.

THE ROLE OF THE PHARMACIST IN PUBLIC HEALTH

The role of the public health pharmacist continues to be defined. The provision of public health pharmacy service is commonplace today. Any person can enter a community pharmacy to seek drug information and obtain assistance in selecting non-prescription medicines to care for common ailments. Any institutional health care worker can request pharmacist consultation for therapeutic drug monitoring or drug information. Few health care professionals routinely offer free services to the public as do pharmacists. Pharmacists have been providing public health services for decades and with greater frequency at present during the pharmaceutical era paradigm.

Historically, pharmacists are among the most trusted health care professionals as a result of the services they provide to society. Pharmacists working in all aspects of health care should incorporate public service into their practices for personal rewards, advancement of the profession, and civic duty.

In the case of macro-level pharmacists, a wide breadth and depth of knowledge is required, which derives from the highly varied nature of their work, usually requiring considerable administrative and organizational skills and often a further qualification. This poses a problem for pharmacy educator who might wish to expose their students to macro-level roles. While the trend in pharmacy education has been away from the drug as a product, it has not been toward administrative and organizational skills, but toward clinical pharmacy practice. Historically, education in pharmacy administration concentrated on drug-store management, marketing, and perhaps accounting. No attention has been given to teaching undergraduates the skills they need to work in health planning agencies, monitor state Medicaid drug programmes, provide in service education, develop health promotional materials, plan community health campaigns, or any of the other specialized tasks performed by pharmacists at the macro-level.

Community activities such as speaking to groups on health-related matters, referring patients to community agencies, participating in community-based programmes on sexually transmitted diseases, mental health, substance abuse, poisoning, and cancer signals, are not regular activities of practicing pharmacists. The most common activities relate to the selection and proper use of drug products. Nevertheless, because of their number and place in the community, the incidence of individual acts of disease prevention and health promotion by pharmacists is significant.

STUDY QUESTIONS

1. What do you mean by Health education?
2. Explain the meaning of Community pharmacy.
3. Discuss the role of the pharmacist in Public health.

■■■

2

Concept of Health

INTRODUCTION

Historically, health and illness were viewed as extremes on a continuum, with the absence of clinically recognizable disease being equated with presence of health. World Health Organization (1974) defined health in terms of well-being and discouraged the conceptualization of health as simply the absence of disease.

Recently W.H.O. modified the definition of health as "a dynamic state of physical, mental, social spiritual wellbeing and not merely absence of disease or infirmity."

W.W. Bauer defines health as 'a state of feeling well in body, mind and spirit together with a sense of reserve power. It is based on normal functioning of tissues and organs of the body, and harmonious adjustment to the physical and psychological environment together with an attitude which regards health is not an end itself, but a means to a richer life as measured in constructive service of mankind'. Thus, good health is based upon the capacity of an individual physical, mental and emotional strengths and takes into account what the individual does during his life.

Dubi equates the states of health within an individual with ability to control his environment and defines health as 'a state of competence of emotional, mental, and physical strength enabling (a person) to set goals, investigate alternatives, make decisions, and take action to control environment'.

Florence Nightingale defined health as being well and using to the fullest extent every power we have. She shows disease as a reparative process that nature instituted because of some want of attention. She also envisioned health as being maintained through prevention of disease via environmental health factors. *Virginia Henderson* assumed that 'health is a quality of life, it is basic to human functions. It requires independence and interdependence. The promotion of health is more important than care of sick. Individuals will achieve or maintain health if they have necessary strength of will or knowledge.'

COMPONENTS OF HEALTH

The three components of health are interrelated and interdependent. A sound body is necessary for a sound mind, and *vice versa*. Persistent and unresolved emotional tensions predispose to somatic diseases. Again, both bodily and mental health are necessary for the proper socialization of the child, and for its acquiring a sound social health. Finally a socially disturbed atmosphere at home (as when the parents are all the time quarrelling) impedes the child's psychological development.

BUILDING OF GOOD HEALTH

Following are the characteristics of a healthy individual:

(i) Emotionally he is stable and does not overreact to pleasant/painful stimuli.

(ii) He is free of pains, aches, discomforts, difficulties (in breathing, eating, urinating, defecating, etc.), depression, disorientation, sores, lumps, bleeding tendencies, and other symptoms.

(iii) In dealing with family members, friends, colleagues, neighbours and others follow the be good and do good principle.

(iv) He can hear and see normally without the aid of gadgets. His other senses (taste, smell, etc.) are adequately developed.

(v) He is heterosexually active and fertile.

(vi) He is whole in body. His weight is normal for his age and height. His height is the average for the community to which he belongs.

(vii) He is of a calm disposition and capable of dealing successfully with stressful situations.

(viii) He has enough manual dexterity to carry out such acts as the use of instruments and implements and the driving of motorized vehicles.

(ix) He is mobile. He can walk, run, climb stairs, jump with ease and elegance.

(x) He falls asleep soon after lying down on the bed and, after 4-6 hours of undisturbed sleep, wakes up refreshed and revitalized.

(xi) All his actions are well within the prescribed legal limits.

(xii) He possesses good language skills and speaking ability. He communicates effectively with others.

(xiii) Now and then, for a few seconds to minutes, he finds his 'self' melting away; his mind and body is filled with the universal principle.

DETERMINANTS OF HEALTH

Determinants of health are the factors that influence the health of a person. These are diverse. Some of the factors relate to the person; these are known as *host factors*. Others are outside the person, and are referred to as the environmental factors. Host determinants are of two types — *Biological factors* are beyond the person's control; examples are age, gender, heredity and race.

Non-biological determinants are the learnt and acquired factors. They depend on training education, stimulation and encouragement the person receives from parents, school teachers, friends and role models—real and fictional. Also they are influenced by the family traditions, food habits, social norms, customs, folkways and more.

Agent Determinants

Pathogenic micro- and macro-organisms, nutrient, dusts, physical factors and chemical substances are the agent determinants. The lodgment of pathogenic micro-organisms followed by their multiplication and toxin elaboration initiates infectious diseases. Lack of nutrients produces deficiency disorders. Chronic inhalation of dusts gives rise to pneumo-coniosis. Ultraviolet rays and ionizing radiation produce somatic and genetic damage. Lead, arsenic, iodine, fluorine are some of the chemicals that affect human health.

Environmental Determinants

Environmental determinants are of two types:

(1) *Physical environmental determinants:* These include, climate, air quality, water quality, soil, natural resources, biological diversity, etc.

(2) *Socio-political environment:* This is made up of all the visible and invisible, tangible and intangible things around a given person at a given moment.

Some of the determinants of health are discussed below:

(i) *Age:* Certain diseases are common in certain age-groups and rare at other ages. Communicable diseases and nutritional deficiencies are common in children. Typhoid, pellagra, Kyasnur Forest Disease and sexually transmitted diseases including AIDS are common in adults. Heart diseases, cancers and chronic degenerative diseases are common in aged individuals.

(ii) *Sex:* Reproductive system disorders are separate for the two sexes. Cardiovascular diseases, cerebro-vascular accidents, Turner's syndrome and haemophilia are common in men whereas schizophrenia, Klienfelter's syndrome, and caries are common in women.

(iii) *Heredity:* Parents who have genetic diseases pass on their defective genes to the progeny. Blood groups inherited from parents are also determinants of health. Persons with blood groups other than A are less susceptible to stomach cancer than those with that blood group.

(iv) *Race:* The dark skin of Negroes protects them against the harmful effects of ultraviolet radiation.

(v) *Immunity:* Infants having maternally transferred antibodies against measles and tetanus do not suffer from these diseases.

(vi) *Nutritional Status and Fitness:* Good nutritional status and a body made strong through regular moderate exercise and/or yoga promote the natural defences of the body and make it resistant to diseases.

(vii) *Life Style:* Those who follow healthy life styles are much healthier than those who follow injured life styles. Some examples of good life styles are washing hands with soap and water before eating, avoidance of excess salt, fats, sweets and cholesterol-containing items, consumption of fiber-rich foods, abstaining from tobacco, alcohol and drugs of addiction, indulgence in safe sex practices, and practicing relaxation techniques.

(viii) *Physical Environment:* Air — both outdoor and indoor — that is free of pollutants, water that is safe for drinking and soil which is free of harmful chemical and parasitological agents are guarantee of good health.

(ix) *Poverty, Unemployment, Bad housing and Illiteracy:* General morbidity and mortality, perinatal mortality, infant mortality and maternal mortality are higher in the poor, the unemployed, the slum-dwellers and the illiterate than in the rich, the well-employed, the dwellers of good houses and the literate.

(x) *Health Services:* Health services that are equitably distributed and easily accessible to all and that lay stress on prevention of diseases promote the health of the population.

(xi) *Child Rearing Practices/Trust:* A few days' delay in commencing breast-feeding deprives the baby of the rich nutrients and protective antibodies that are in abundance in colostrums, and thus makes it prone to suffer from infections. Failure to shower love and affection on the child, too much or too less disciplinary control over him, and lack of parent-child communication and interaction lead to the child developing psychological and sociopathic conditions. Interpersonal interactions based on trust and goodwill promote health.

INDICATORS OF HEALTH

Following are the important statistical indices of a country's health status:

(i) Crude birth-rate.
(ii) Crude death-rate.
(iii) Specific death-rates.
(iv) Standardised death-rates.
(v) Proportional mortality-rate.
(vi) Age proportional mortality-rates.
(vii) Maternal mortality-rate.
(viii) Infant mortality-rate.
(ix) Neo-natal and post-neonatal mortality-rates.
(x) Percentage of low birth-weight babies.
(xi) Perinatal mortality-rate.
(xii) Pre-school child mortality-rate.
(xiii) Life expectancy.
(xiv) Disability days.
(xv) Sullivan's index.
(xvi) Physical quality of life index.
(xvii) Disability adjusted life years.
(xviii) Blindness incidence rate.
(xix) Human development index.

MAINTENANCE OF HEALTH

Health maintenance is the preventive, curative, restorative and promotive service provided by the official and non-official agencies of a country to its citizens. Health maintenance is the job not of a single man, but of a large number of paramedical and allied workers. They work not in isolation but together as a team. Until the British rule, health care in India was ill-organised and based on Unani/ Tibbi, Avurveda, Siddha and Naturopathy systems of medicine.

After the advent of the British rule and up to 1952, the health care was predominantly curative care based on allopathy. It was available chiefly to the city/town dwellers and the rich. The providers of healthcare were culturally at a different wavelength than the beneficiaries. The people never participated in the health programmes.

FACTORS OF HEALTH AND DISEASES

The factors that influence health and illness related to the person in terms of the human dimensions are as follows:

Each person is a composite of physical dimension, emotional dimension, environmental dimension, intellectual dimensions, social-cultural dimensions and spiritual dimension, and each dimension influences the behaviour of the person receiving care.

Physical dimension: It includes genetic makeup, age, developmental level, race, and sex. All are parts of individuals, which strongly influence health status, and health practices.

Emotional dimension: It expresses that how the mind and body interact to affect body function.

DISEASE

A disease or medical condition is an abnormal condition of an organism that impairs bodily functions and can be deadly. It is also defined as a way of the body harming itself in an abnormal way, associated with specific symptoms and signs.

In human beings, "disease" is often used more broadly to refer to any condition that causes extreme pain, dysfunction, distress, social problems, and/or death to the person afflicted, or similar problems for those in contact with the person. In this broader sense, it sometimes includes injuries, disabilities, disorders, syndromes, infections, isolated symptoms, deviant behaviours, and atypical variations of structure and function, while in other contexts and for other purposes these may be considered distinguishable categories.

TRANSMISSION OF DISEASE

Some diseases such as influenza are contagious and infectious. Infectious diseases can be transmitted by as, by hand to mouth contact with infectious material on surfaces, by bites of insects or other carriers of the disease, and from contaminated water or food (often via faecal contamination), etc. In addition, there are sexually transmitted diseases. In some cases, micro-organisms that are not readily spread from person to person play a role, while other diseases can be prevented or ameliorated with appropriate nutrition or other lifestyle changes. Some diseases such as cancer, heart disease and mental disorders are , in most cases, not considered to be caused by infection, although there are important exceptions. Many diseases (including some cancers, heart disease and mental disorders) have a partially or completely genetic basis.

HEALTH-DISEASE SPECTRUM

The transition from health to disease, or from disease to health is not abrupt but gradual: it occurs through stages or phases. These stages constitute the *health-disease spectrum*. At one extreme is the optimum, ideal or positive health, a state of health beyond which no improvement is possible. Next is the stage of 'sub-optimum' health. A person in this stage is healthy and has no pathological abnormality, but his condition is capable of improvement.

Third is the stage of 'sub-clinical' disease. An individual in this stage no doubt is diseased; but there is nothing that matters with him. The physician who examines him clinically fails to detect any abnormality. The disease is capable of detection with the aid of laboratory tests. The sub-clinical stage may be absent in the cases of some diseases.

From the sub-clinical stage, the person may revert to sub-optimum health, or, on the contrary, pass on to the fourth stage called the 'overt' stage. The disease is now at its zenith. A diagnosis can be readily made on clinical examination.

The last, the most undesirable, stage is that of *'advanced' disease*. The disease is now at its worst; also often it is associated with complications. Beyond advanced disease is the realm of death.

An illness is the response, the person has, to a *disease*; it is an abnormal process in which the person's level of functioning is changed compared with a previous level. Disease is a medical term meaning that there is pathological change in the structure or function of the body or mind. It is a condition that has specific symptoms and boundaries where health and illness are individualized perceptions and definitions of oneself.

(i) *Culture:* It represents non-physical traits, such as values, belief, attitudes and customs shared by a group of people and passed from one generation to the next. Culture is also the sum of beliefs, practices, habits, likes, dislikes, norms, customs and rituals learned from family during the years of socialization.

(ii) *Ethnicity:* It is a sense of identification associated with a cultural group's common social and cultural heritage. The characteristics of an ethnic group include common language, and dialect, migratory states, race, and religious faith, and practices. People share traditions, values symbols, literature, folklore, music and food preference.

(iii) *Religion*: It is a belief in divine or superhuman power (or powers) to be obeyed and worshipped as the creator and ruler of the universe. Religious teachings help formulate a meaningful philosophy and system of practices through the system of beliefs, practices, and social controls having specific values, norms and ethics that vary between religious groups.

(iv) *Illness*: It is not merely the presence of disease process. Illness is a state in which a person's physical, emotional, intellectual, social, developmental or spiritual functioning is diminished or impaired, compared with that person's experience.

Illness behaviour involves the ways persons monitor their bodies, define and interpret their symptoms, take remedial measures/ actions and the use of healthcare systems.

It also can serve as a coping mechanism. It may be a means of obtaining reassurance. Clients may need reassurance that the inability to care for themselves is due to physical disease. Illness behaviour can result in clients being released from roles, social expectations or responsibilities.

PHASES OF DISEASES

PATHOGENESIS

The phase *pathogenesis* means step by step development of a disease due to a series of changes in the structure and /or function of a cell/tissue/organ being caused by a microbial, chemical or physical agent. The pathogenesis of a disease is the mechanism by which an etiological factor causes the disease. The term can also be used to describe the development of the disease, such as acute, chronic and recurrent. The word comes from the Greek pathos, "disease", and genesis, "creation".

Types of pathogenesis include *microbial infection, inflammation, malignancy,* and *tissue breakdown*. Most diseases are caused by multiple pathogenetical processes together. For example, certain cancers arise from dysfunction of the immune system (skin tumors and lymphoma after a renal transplant, which requires immuno-suppression). Often, a potential etiology is identified by epidemiological observations before a pathological link can be drawn between the cause and the disease.

PREPATHOGENESIS

The phase *prepathogenesis* is the stage before the onset of disease in man. The causative factors of diseases are—*agent, host* and *environment.*

(i) Agents

It is defined as a living or non-living susbtance which may initiate a disease process. They may be categories as:

(i) *Biological agents* are living organisms, e.g., protozoa, fungi, bacteria and virus.

(ii) *Chemical agents* may be exogenous or endogenous produce in the body, e.g., fumes, dusts and gases present outside the body means *exogenous.* Urea, uric acid etc. are endogenous agents.

(iii) *Nutrient agents* are those agents which spread disease either by excess or deficiency of nutrients. Nutrient agents are proteins, fats, carbohydrates, vitamins and minerals.

(iv) *Mechanical agents* spread disease through mechanical forces, e.g., crushing, tearing, sprains and even in death.

(v) *Social agents* are smoking, poverty, drug abuse, alcohol unhealthy life-style etc.

(ii) Host

A host is an organism that harbors a virus or parasite, or a mutual or commensal symbiont, typically providing nourishment and shelter. In botany, a host plant is one that supplies food resources and substrate for certain insects or other fauna. Examples of such interactions include a cell being host to a virus, a legume plant hosting helpful nitrogen-fixing bacteria, and animals as hosts to parasitic worms, e.g., nematodes.

A ***primary host*** or definitive host is a host in which the parasite reaches maturity and, if applicable, reproduces sexually.

A ***secondary host*** or intermediate host is a host that harbors the parasite only for a short transition period, during which (usually) some developmental stage is completed. For trypanosomes, the cause of sleeping sickness, humans are the primary host, while the tsetse fly is the secondary host. Cestodes (tapeworms) and other parasitic flatworms have complex life-cycles, in which specific developmental stages are completed in a sequence of several different hosts.

As the ***life cycles*** of many parasites are not well understood, sometimes the "more important" organism is arbitrarily defined as definitive, and this designation may continue even after it is determined to be incorrect. For example, sludge worms are sometimes considered "*intermediate hosts*" for whirling disease, even though it is known that the parasite causing the disease reproduces sexually inside them.

In Trichinella spiralis, the roundworm that causes trichinosis, a host has both reproductive adult in its digestive tract and immature juveniles in its muscles, and is therefore considered both an intermediate host and a definitive host.

A *paratenic host* is similar to an intermediate host, only that it is not needed for the parasite's development cycle to progress. There are also reservoir hosts. A *reservoir* can harbor a pathogen indefinitely with no ill effects. A single reservoir host may be reinfected several times. The difference between a paratenic and reservoir host is that the latter is a primary host, whereas paratenic hosts serve as "dumps" for non-mature stages of a parasite which they can accumulate in high numbers.

A dead-end host is an intermediate host that does generally not allow transmission to the definite host, thereby preventing the parasite from completing its development. For example, humans are dead-end hosts for Echinococcus canine tapeworms. As infected humans are not usually eaten by dogs, foxes etc., the immature Echinococcus — although it causes serious disease in the dead-end host — is unable to infect the primary host and mature.

Host Range

The host range or host specificity of a parasite is the collection of hosts that an organism can utilize as a partner. In the case of *human parasites,* the host range influences the epidemiology of the *parasitism* or *disease*. For instance, the production of antigenic shifts in Influenza A *virus* can result from pigs being infected with the virus from several different hosts (such as human and bird). This co-infection provides an opportunity for mixing of the viral genes between existing strains, thereby producing a new viral strain. An influenza vaccine produced against an existing viral strain might not be effective against this new strain, which then requires a new influenza vaccine to be prepared for the protection of the human population.

(iii) Environment

The biophysical environment is the symbiosis between the physical environment and the biological life forms within the environment, and include all variables that comprise the Earth's biosphere. The environment in which man lives is an important factor in the causation of diseases. They may be—

Physical environment: It refers to physical factors such as air, water, light etc. Physical environment produces a variety of diseases, e.g., air pollution, water pollution, noise pollution etc.

Biological environment include man and living things such as bacteria, viruses, insect and animals which produce various types of diseases.

Psychological environment includes habits, attitudes, culture, customs, life-style etc.

CONCEPT OF PREVENTION OF DISEASES

In medicine, prevention is any activity which reduces the burden of mortality or morbidity from disease. This takes place at primary, secondary and tertiary prevention levels.

Primary prevention avoids the development of a disease. Most population-based health promotion activities are primary preventive measures.

Secondary prevention activities are aimed at early disease detection, thereby increasing opportunities for interventions to prevent progression of the disease and emergence of symptoms.

Tertiary prevention reduces the negative impact of an already established disease by restoring function and reducing disease-related complications.

DIFFERENCE BETWEEN PREVENTIONS, TREATMENTS, AND CURES

A ***prevention*** or preventive measure is a way to avoid an injury, sickness, or disease in the first place, and generally it will not help someone who is already ill (though there are exceptions). For instance, many American babies are given a polio vaccination soon after they are born, which prevents them from contracting polio. But the vaccination does not work on patients who already have polio. A treatment or cure is applied after a medical problem has already started.

A ***treatment*** treats a problem, and may lead to its cure, but treatments more often ameliorate a problem only for as long as the treatment is continued. For example, there is no cure for AIDS, but treatments are available to slow down the harm done by HIV and delay the fatality of the disease. Treatments don't always work. For example, chemotherapy is a treatment for cancer which may cure the disease, sometimes — it does not have a 100% cure rate. Therefore, chemotherapy isn't considered a bonafide cure for cancer.

Cures are a subset of treatments that reverse illnesses completely or end medical problems permanently. In the area of substance-related harms, a number of prevention typologies have been proposed.

HEALTH PROMOTION

Health promotion, as defined by the World Health Organization, is the process of enabling people to increase control over, and to improve, their health. Health promotion is much more narrowly conceived as "the science and art of helping people change their life-style to move toward a state of optimal health." Means of health promotion include health education and social marketing. According to the *Ottawa Charter* for Health Promotion the basic principles of health promotion are:

Prerequisites for Health

The fundamental conditions and resources for health are peace, shelter, education, food, income, a stable ecosystem, sustainable resources, social justice and equity. Improvement in health requires a secure foundation in these basic prerequisites.

Advocate

Good health is a major resource for social, economic and personal development and an important dimension of quality of life. Political, economic, social, cultural, environmental, behavioural and biological factors can all favour health or be harmful to it. Health promotion action aims at making these conditions favourable through advocacy for health.

Enable

Health promotion focuses on achieving equity in health. Health promotion action aims at reducing differences in current health status and ensuring equal opportunities and resources to enable all people to achieve their fullest health potential. This includes a secure foundation in a supportive environment, access to information, life skills and opportunities for making healthy choices. People cannot achieve their fullest health potential unless they are able to take control of those things which determine their health. This must apply equally to women and men.

Mediate

The prerequisites and prospects for health cannot be ensured by the health sector alone. More importantly, health promotion demands coordinated action by all concerned: by governments, by health and other social and economic sectors, by non-governmental and voluntary organizations, by local authorities, by industry and by the media. People in all walks of life are involved as individuals, families and communities. Professional and social groups and health personnel have a major responsibility to mediate between differing interests in society for the pursuit of health.

Health promotion strategies and programmes should be adapted to the local needs and possibilities of individual countries and regions to take into account differing social, cultural and economic systems.

Build Healthy Public Policy

Health promotion goes beyond healthcare. It puts health on the agenda of policy-makers in all sectors and at all levels, directing them to be aware of the health consequences of their decisions and to accept their responsibilities for health.

Health promotion policy combines diverse but complementary approaches including legislation, fiscal measures, taxation and organizational change. It is coordinated action that leads to health, income and social policies that foster greater equity. Joint action contributes to ensuring safer and healthier goods and services, healthier public services, and cleaner, more enjoyable environments.

Health promotion policy requires the identification of obstacles to the adoption of healthy public policies in non-health sectors, and ways of removing them. The aim must be to make the healthier choice the easier choice for policy-makers as well.

Create Supportive Environments

Societies are complex and interrelated. Health cannot be separated from other goals. The inextricable links between people and their environment constitute the basis for a socioecological approach to health. The overall guiding principle for the world, nations, regions and communities alike is the need to encourage reciprocal maintenance — to take care of each other, our communities and our natural environment. The conservation of natural resources throughout the world should be emphasized as a global responsibility.

Changing patterns of life, work and leisure have a significant impact on health. Work and leisure should be a source of health for people. The way society organizes work should help create a healthy society. Health promotion generates living and working conditions that are safe, stimulating, satisfying and enjoyable.

Systematic assessment of the health impact of a rapidly changing environment — particularly in areas of technology, work, energy production and urbanization is essential and must be followed by action to ensure positive benefit to the health of the public. The protection of the natural and built environments and the conservation of natural resources must be addressed in any health promotion strategy.

Strengthen Community Action

Health promotion works through concrete and effective community action in setting priorities, making decisions, planning strategies and implementing them to achieve better health. At the heart of this process is the empowerment of communities, their ownership and control of their own endeavours and destinies.

Community development draws on existing human and material resources in the community to enhance self-help and social support, and to develop flexible systems for strengthening public participation and direction of health matters. This requires full and continuous access to information, learning opportunities for health, as well as funding support.

Develop Personal Skills

Health promotion supports personal and social development through providing information, education for health and enhancing life skills. By so doing, it increases the options available to people to exercise more control over their own health and over their environments, and to make choices conducive to health.

Enabling people to learn throughout life, to prepare themselves for all of its stages and to cope with chronic illness and injuries is essential. This has to be facilitated in school, home, work and community settings. Action is required through educational, professional, commercial and voluntary bodies, and within the institutions themselves.

Reorient Health Services

The responsibility for health promotion in health services is shared among individuals, community groups, health professionals, health service institutions and governments. They must work together towards a healthcare system which contributes to the pursuit of health.

The role of the health sector must move increasingly in a health promotion direction, beyond its responsibility for providing clinical and curative services. Health services need to embrace an expanded mandate which is sensitive and respects cultural needs. This mandate should support the needs of individuals and communities for a healthier life, and open channels between the health sector and broader social, political, economic and physical environmental components.

Reorienting health services also requires stronger attention to health research as well as changes in professional education and training. This must lead to a change of attitude and organization of health services, which refocuses on the total needs of the individual as a whole person.

REHABILITATION

It is also called *rehab*. After a serious injury, illness or surgery, you may recover slowly. You may need to regain your strength, relearn skills or find new ways of doing things you did before. This process is *rehabilitation*. Rehabilitation often focuses on:

- *Physical therapy* to help your strength, mobility and fitness.
- *Occupational therapy* to help you with your daily activities.

- *Speech-language therapy* to help with speaking, understanding, reading, writing and swallowing.
- *Treatment of pain.*

The type of therapy and goals of therapy may be different for different people. For example, an older person who has had a stroke may simply want to dress or bathe without help. The goal of younger person who has suffered a heart attack may be to return to work and normal activities.

According to the *National Institute of Heatlh*, a *clinical trial* (also clinical research) is a research study in human *volunteers* to answer specific health questions. Carefully conducted clinical trials are the fastest and safest way to find treatments that work in people and ways to improve health. Interventional trials determine whether experimental treatments or new ways of using known therapies are safe and effective under controlled environments. Observational trials address health issues in large groups of people or populations in natural settings.

Rehabilitation of people with ***disabilities*** is a process aimed at enabling them to reach and maintain their optimal physical, sensory, intellectual, psychological and social functional levels. Rehabilitation provides disabled people with the tools they need to attain independence and self-determination.

Drug rehabilitation (often drug *rehab* or just *rehab*) is an umbrella term for the processes of medical and/or psychotherapeutic treatment, for dependency on psychoactive substances such as alcohol, prescription drugs, and so-called street drugs such as cocaine, heroin or amphetamines. The general intent is to enable the patient to cease substance abuse, in order to avoid the psychological, legal, financial, social, and physical consequences that can be caused, especially by extreme abuse.

Occupational therapy, often abbreviated as "OT", incorporates meaningful and purposeful occupation to enable people with limitations or impairments to participate in everyday life. Occupational therapists work with individuals, families, groups and populations to facilitate health and well-being through engagement or re-engagement in occupation. Occupational therapists are becoming increasingly involved in addressing the impact of social and environmental factors that contribute to exclusion and occupational deprivation.

Neurocognitive rehabilitation is a rehabilitation methodology addressed to many disabilities; it's particularly utilized for cognitive and/or motricity diseases.

Physical therapy, the physiotherapy in most English-speaking countries, is a health-care profession which provides services to individuals and populations to develop, maintain and restore maximum movement and functional ability throughout the life-span. This includes providing services in circumstances where movement and function are threatened by aging, injury, disease or environmental factors. Functional movement is central to what it means to be healthy.

Physical medicine and rehabilitation (PM&R), or physiatry, is a branch of medicine dealing with functional restoration of a person affected by physical disability. A physician who has completed training in this field is referred to as a psychiatric. In order to be a physiatrist in the United States, one must complete four years of medical school, one year of internship and three years of residency. Physiatrists specialize in restoring optimal function to people with injuries to the muscles, bones, tissues, and nervous system (such as stroke patients).

Rehabilitation of sensory and cognitive function typically involves methods for retraining neural pathways or training new neural pathways to regain or improve neurocognitive functioning that has been diminished by disease or traumatic injury.

Three common neuropsychological problems treatable with rehabilitation are attention deficit/hyperactivity disorder (ADHD), concussion, and spinal cord injury.

Stroke rehabilitation, or, in more optimistic terms, stroke recovery, is the process by which patients with disabling strokes undergo treatment to help them return to normal life as much as possible by regaining and relearning the skills of everyday living. It is multidisciplinary in that it involves a team with different skills working together to help the patient. These include nursing staff, physiotherapy, occupational therapy, speech and language therapy and usually a physician trained in rehabilitation medicine. Some teams may also include psychologists and social workers and pharmacists. Patients may demand access to state of the art treatment with the help of their own doctor.

Vocational rehabilitation, the continuous and coordinated process of rehabilitation which involves the provision of vocational guidance, vocational training and selective placement, designed to enable a person with a disability to secure and retain suitable employment.

STUDY QUESTIONS

1. Explain the Concept of Health. What are the main components of Health?
2. Write short notes on the following:
   (a) Transmission of disease;
   (b) Health-disease spectrum;
   (c) Phases of diseases; and
   (d) Health promotion.

■■■

3

Health and Nutrition

INTRODUCTION

Nutrition is the science that deals with all the various factors of which food is composed and the way in which proper nourishment is brought about. The average nutritional requirements of groups of people are fixed and depend on such measurable characteristics such as age, sex, height, weight, degree of activity and rate of growth.

Food is anything solid or liquid that has a chemical composition which enables it, when swallowed to do one or more of the following:

- Provide the body with the material from which it can produce heat, or any form of energy.
- Provide material to allow growth, maintenance, repair or reproduction to proceed.
- Supply substances, which normally regulate the production of energy or the process of growth, repair or reproduction.

Good nutrition requires a satisfactory diet, which is capable of supporting the individual consuming it, in a state of good health by providing the desired nutrients in required amounts. It must provide the right amount of fuel to execute normal physical activity. If the total amount of nutrients provided in the diet is insufficient, a state of undernutrition will develop.

NUTRITION AND HEALTH

Good nutrition requires a satisfactory diet, which is capable of supporting the individual consuming it, in a state of good health by providing the desired nutrients in required amounts. It must provide the right amount of fuel to execute normal physical activity. If the total amount of nutrients provided in the diet is insufficient, a state of undernutrition will develop.

Nutrition is one key to developing and maintaining a state of health that is optimal for you. In addition, a poor diet coupled with a sedentary life-style is known to be risk factor for life-threatening chronic diseases and death: Heart disease, Stroke, Hypertension, Diabetes and some forms of Cancer.

Health is defined by the World Health Organization of the United Nations as the "State of complete physical, mental and social well-being and not merely the absence of disease and infirmity (or ill-health/illness)".

CLASSIFICATION OF FOOD

The energy value of food is measured in terms of heat units called *calories*. Foods are classified according to their functions under the following heads :

(a) *Protective foods:* These are foods rich in protein, vitamins, minerals and water, e.g., milk, egg, liver, green leafy vegetables, fruits, legumes. They provide material for repair in the body as wear and tear goes on constantly and are required for the maintenance and regulation of tissue functions.

(b) *Energy producing foods:* These foods are rich in carbohydrates and fats, e.g., cereals, sugar, honey, jellies. They supply heat and energy to the body.

(c) *Body-building foods:* These are foods rich in proteins, e.g., meat, fish, pulses, oilseeds, eggs, nuts, milk. These are anabolic foods, required for body-building.

Foodstuffs may be broadly classified as the following:

1. Cereals, e.g., rice, *ragi*, wheat, maize, jowar, etc., which produce carbohydrates.
2. Pulses, which give proteins.
3. Nuts and oilseed, e.g., groundnut, almond, cashewnut, mustard seed, soyabean, etc. provide protein and fat.
4. Vegetables, e.g., green leafy vegetables (spinach, amaranth which provide carotene), root vegetables, e.g., tapioca, potato, sweet potato, etc. provide carbohydrate, other vegetables (brinjal, lady finger, french beans) which provide vitamins.
5. Fruits, e.g., guavas, amia, citrus fruits, etc. provide vitamins. Mangoes, orange, papaya, etc. provide carotene. Dried fruits like dates and raisins provide iron.
6. Milk and milk products, e.g., milk, curds, cheese, which provide proteins.
7. Flesh foods, e.g., fish, poultry, meat provide class proteins.

BALANCED DIET

Balanced diet is a diet that contains carbohydrates, proteins, fats, minerals, vitamins, and water in correct proportions, and in quantity adequate for current requirement as well as for the needs in future emergencies. It satisfies the energy requirement of the person.

As a rough guide the balanced diet consists of 60% items from the vegetable kingdom. Preferably cereals should comprise two or more of rice, wheat, jowar, bajra and *ragi*. Locally available and seasonal GLV and fruits (that are cheap) are included in the diet. For a non-vegetarian, one egg, or 30 G of fish or meat, and an extra 5 G of fat, oil or vanaspathi replace 50% of pulses.

Elderly individuals of both sexes require 100 G of GLV and 200 G of milk and milk products, and 20 G each of sugar or jaggery and fats or oils. Elderly men require 325 G, and women, 270 G of cereals. Requirement of other items is as for a sedentary adult man. During the second half of pregnancy and lactation, women require the following additional allowances:

RULES OF PRUDENT DIET

Following are the rules of prudent diet; these rules are sometimes referred to as dietary goals:

1. Proteins should constitute 15-20% of the food intake.
2. Total fats should constitute 20-30% of the food intake. But saturated type of fats should be limited to 10% of the energy requirement.
3. Not more than 5 G of salt per day should be consumed.
4. The following should be avoided:
   (a) Highly refined carbohydrates like sugar, jaggery, candy, sweets, toffees, chocolates, honey, etc.
   (b) Junk foods like burgers, fries, pizzas, bottled cool drinks, ketchup, packed salted snacks, etc.

BASIC FOOD PRODUCTS

1. Cereals

The common cereals are rice, wheat, maize, barley, rye, oats and millets. The millets consist of jowar, bajra, and *ragi*. The bulk of man's food (staple diet) consists of one kind or other of cereals. Cereals are monocotyledons or single-grained seeds of the domesticated grasses. As harvested they are enclosed in a woody envelope called husk that is removed by milling.

The grain itself is spherical, ovoid or spindle-shaped varying in size from 0.5 mm in the case of *ragi* to 10 mm in the case of maize. The grain is divisible into four parts: germ (embryo) which is situated at the pole; bran, the outer protective covering; endosperm or the inner kernel forming 75% to 80% of the grain; and scutellum, the portion between the germ and endosperm.

2. Rice

Rice is the seed of *Oryza sativa*. Different natural as well as hybrid varieties are grown. The protein of rice is of better quality than that of wheat as it has less deficiency of lysine — an essential amino acid — than wheat. Iron and phosphorus are the important minerals in rice. However, iron is not available to the body because it combines with phytic acid (also present in rice) and is excreted in the faeces. Among the cereals rice has the lowest amount of calcium. The outer coat of rice is a good source of thiamine, niacin, pyridoxine and riboflavin. Rice does not contain vitamin A (or its precursors) and vitamin C.

3. Wheat

Wheat is the seed of *Triticum sativum*. Unlike rice, which is cooked as such, wheat is first ground to rava, flour or maida. Gluten, the wheat protein, lacks in lysine and is inferior to rice-protein. It is sticky and thus enables the flour to be made into bread.

Wheat is a good source of calcium,. phosphorus, iron and other minerals. However, they are not properly absorbed because of their interaction with phytic and oxalic acids. Wheat supplies thiamine, niacin and riboflavin.

4. Pulses or Legumes

Pulses (from 'puls', thick soup) are the dry seeds of leguminous plants. They are dicotyledons. A series of seeds are enclosed in a pod. Seeds, varied in hue, are spherical or ovoid, 2-10 mm in diameter. Pulses are used either as whole, or split into halves, called *dais* (dhals): Bengal gram (chana), green gram (moong), red gram (tur), black gram (urad), lentil (masur), and soyabeans are the common pulses.

Pulse proteins are deficient in the amino acids methionine and tryptophane. Soyabeans have 43% proteins, 20% fats, and 20% carbohydrates. Their protein is qualitatively the best among the vegetable proteins. Because of their high protein content, pulses are referred to as the poor man's beef. Whole pulses are good source of iron, calcium, sulfur and potassium. Unfortunately most of these combine with phytic and oxalic acids and are not absorbed. Whole grains contain thiamine, niacin, riboflavin and pyridoxine. Sprouted ones (germinating seeds) contain vitamin C too.

5. Nuts and Oilseeds

Nuts are seeds enclosed in a hard shell: hazelnut, chestnut, walnut, almond, and pistachio. Oilseeds are a miscellaneous group used for the extraction of oil: groundnuts, coconut, sesame (til or gingelly), sunflower seeds, safflower seeds (kusum or kardi), linseed, and rapeseed. Coconut is not a nut but a stone fruit.

Groundnuts (peanuts, monkey nuts or goober) are actually pulses, being the underground fruits of a leguminous plant, Arachis hypogaea. They contain 27% protein, 25% carbohydrates, 40% fats and 2% minerals. Thiamine, niacin and riboflayin are present in groundnuts. The groundnut protein, predominantly 'arachin', lacks methionine and lysine. Groundnut cake is what is left of groundnuts after oil has been extracted. It contains 41% protein and 39% carbohydrates. Unfortunately, it is used as non-human (cattle) food.

6. Green Leafy Vegetables (GLVs)

Popular GLVs are fenugreek (methi), mint (pudina), spinach (palak), coriander (kothmir), amaranth (raj girha), and lettuce. Cabbage is a leafy vegetable but is not green.

GLVs are poor in carbohydrates (2-10%) and poorer in proteins (0.5%). On the other hand, they are a good source of minerals — calcium, iron, sodium, chlorides and vitamins — ascorbic acid, thiamine, riboflavin and folates. They do not contain vitamin A as such, but contain its precursor, beta-carotene. They afford flavour to food. The cellulose in them provides roughage and helps the motility of the large intestines. In addition, GLVs help maintain the blood alkalinity.

7. Roots, Tubers and Other Vegetables

Examples of roots and tubers are potato, carrot, yam, colocasia, sago, radish and tapioca. Other vegetables include brinjal, cauliflower, lady-finger, pumpkin, cucumber, bitter gourd and ridge gourd.

Roots and tubers have 10-20%, and other vegetables 3-8%, carbohydrates. Both groups have only 0.5% proteins. Their importance lies in the fact that they contain minerals—calcium, phosphorus and iron—and vitamins, particularly beta carotene and ascorbic acid.

8. Fruits

Fruits such as banana, mango, papaya, orange, grapes, etc., contain 70-90% water, negligible fats and proteins, and 5-20% carbohydrates in the form of fructose and sucrose. The riper the fruit, the greater the carbohydrate content.

Fruits are good source of iron, calcium, sodium and potassium. They contain beta-carotene, thiamine and ascorbic acid. They promote the movements of the large intestines and thus exhibit laxative properties. Finally, they help maintain acid-base equilibrium of the body fluids.

9. Meat and Edible Organs

Meat is the skeletal muscle of animals and such birds as chicken, pigeon and duck. The common edible organs are tongue, liver, kidney, thymus, brain and heart.

Meat contains 18-22% proteins, 10-20% fats, and 1.5% minerals. It does not contain carbohydrates. The proteins of meat are myosin, myoalbumin and haemoglobin. They are of high biological value as they contain all the essential amino acids in the right proportions. The minerals of note in meat are iron, phosphorus and potassium. Liver contains thiamine, niacin, cyanocobalamin, and vitamins A and D. Meat is poor in all vitamins except thiamine and niacin.

10. Fish

Fish are aquatic scaly vertebrates possessing fins and gills. Some of them are found in sea, others in fresh waters. Most are edible but a few are poisonous. Fish contain 15-20% protein of high biological value. 'Lean' fish contain less than 2%, and 'fat' fish, 2-10% of fat. Fish do not contain carbohydrates. Calcium (present in bones), phosphorus, manganese, iron and copper are the minerals found in fish. Salt-water fish contain iodine and fluorine too. Fish are good source of vitamins A and D, thiamine, niacin, riboflavin and cyanocobalamin.

11. Egg

Eggs of hen, duck and turkey are commonly eaten. They contain 13.3% each of proteins and fats, 1% minerals and no carbohydrates. Protein in the form of ovalbumin is present in the outer white part. It is of high biological value (reference protein). A little protein (vitellin) occurs in the yellow part called yolk. Fat of egg is present in the yolk.

12. Milk

Milk (mammary secretion) of cows, buffaloes, goats, and occasionally, of ass, mare, yak, camel, and reindeer, is consumed. Milk is free of peculiar smell and taste. Its specific gravity lies between 1028 and 1032. On chemical analysis it has at least 3% fat and at least 8.5% "solids not fat (SNF)", in the case of cow's milk, and 6% fat and 9% SNF in that of buffalo's milk. With methylene blue reduction test, it takes at least 42 hours to reduce the dye. On microscopic examination it has less than 500,000 cells/ml.

Pasteurized milk is the milk subjected to "pasteurization", a process of heating milk to a temperature below its boiling point, for a definite period, and then chilling it to 50°C.

If milk has been adequately pasteurized, the "phosphatase test" will be negative, because the enzyme phosphatase in milk gets destroyed at the temperature-time combination employed for pasteurization.

Both boiling and pasteurization destroy the pathogenic organisms in milk. The advantages of pasteurization of milk over boiling are these: (a) It does not affect the taste of milk; and (b) It results in less loss of iodine, calcium and phosphorus.

NUTRIENTS

Nutrients are also called *nutriments.* Nutrients are foods that contain the necessary elements, which perform various functions in the body. There are six categories of nutrients— carbohydrates, proteins, fats, vitamins, minerals, and water. Further, these nutrients can be groups as macronutrients and micronutrients.

(i) *Macronutrients:* These are those which the body requires in relatively large amounts. Proteins, fats and carbohydrates are called *macronutrients* as they form the main bulk of food.

(ii) *Micronutrients:* These are those which the body requires in small quantities. Vitamins and minerals are known as *micronutrients* due to their requirement in small quantity.

CARBOHYDRATES

Carbohydrates are the compounds of carbon, hydrogen and oxygen. These compounds can be classified as monosaccharides, disaccharides or polysaccharides.

The *monosaccharides* include sugar like glucose, fructose and glactose. The other type of sugars, i.e., *disaccharides* are sucrose, lactose and maltose. The *polysaccharides* include starch, cellulose, etc.

(i) *Sources:* Cereals, millets, roots, tubers, cane sugar, beetroot, fruits.

(ii) *Uses:* They provide energy and heat. These act as a protein spares. Excess of carbohydrate is converted into fat. These are required for synthesis of certain non-essential amino-acids. They provide 4 kcals per gram of carbohydrate.

GOOD CARBOHYDRATES

Carbohydrate (meaning "carbon plus water") is the most widely eaten food in the world. Along with fat and protein, carbohydrate is an essential nutrient, but what makes carbs different is that they are easily converted to energy by the body. Also, glucose, the simplest carbohydrate, is essential fuel for the brain. Any healthy diet must include carbohydrates.

1. Fruit and Vegetables

Fruit and vegetables are generally low in calories and packed with nutrients like vitamins, minerals, phytochemicals and fiber.

2. Whole Grains

This group includes *pasta, rice* and *noodles* — the starchy carbohydrates — your body's main source of energy. All these foods begin life as a grain, such as wheat, rye, corn, rice or barley.

3. Potatoes

Another high-starch carbohydrate, potatoes have higher GI values. New white potatoes (fresh or canned) are better choices, with sweet potatoes being best of all. Potatoes are a fat-free healthy food that provide useful amounts of vitamin C, potassium and fiber. Their high GI value can be reduced by eating them with other low-GI foods as part of the same meal.

How Much Carbohydrate Do We Need in Our Daily Diet?

Assuming you choose nutritious less refined carbohydrates, you can eat anything between 40 and 60 percent of your calories in the form of carbs. If you wish to try a low-carb diet, that's fine — but for optimum health you should avoid the very-low-carb weight loss plans except for very short periods of time. Some of these very-low-carb diets rely on nutritional supplements, which generally speaking is not a good long term dietary habit to adopt.

PROTEINS

Proteins are the basic units of the body which are required for nutrition, growth and repair, and affect a huge number of metabolic, enzyme and chemical processes that occur inside the body. Proteins are complex organic nitrogenous compounds consisting of carbon, hydrogen, sulphur and occasionally phosphorous. Human body contains 16% protein. They are made up of a number of smaller units called *amino acids*. These amino acids are classified as :

Essential amino acids, e.g., leucine, isoleucine, methionine, tryptophan, phenyl alanine, threonine, valine, lysine and histidine. They cannot be synthesized in the body and must be included in the diet.

Non-essential amino acids, e.g., Arginine, asparagine, cysteine, glutamic acid, proline, glycine. They can be synthesized by the body.

(i) *Sources:* Milk, egg, meat, fish, beef, pulses, cereals, legumes, nuts, fruits etc.

(ii) *1st class proteins:* Protein foods which contains all the essential amino acids in correct proportions – meat, egg, fish, soyabean, milk.

(iii) *2nd class proteins:* They do not contain all the essential amino acids in the correct proportion – peas, beans, pulses.

(iv) *Uses:* Proteins are required for body building, repair and maintenance of body tissues. These are required for biosynthesis of plasma proteins, haemoglobin, antibodies, enzymes and hormones. These play an important role in the constitution of all tissues including body fluids, e.g., blood. These provide energy and heat. These are responsible for the cell-mediated immune response.

As per the recommendation of *Indian Council of Medical Research* (ICMR) the daily protein requirement for an adult is 1.0 gm per kilogram body weight. However, protein requirements are affected in growing children, pregnancy, lactation, burns, surgery, diabetes, worm infestation, emotional disturbances.

Best Protein Food Choices Are Proteins Low in Saturates

Protein may come in many forms, but the better type of protein is low in saturated fat. Good protein choices include: fish, lean beef, lean ham, egg whites, whole eggs, chicken breast, turkey breast, pulses, beans, nuts, seeds, soy products and vegetarian protein foods.

How Much Protein Do We Need in Our Diet?

Assuming you choose nutritious protein, low in saturated fat, you can eat anything between 10 and 20 percent of your calories in the form of protein, although according to government guidelines you should not eat less than 45 g of protein (adult females) or 55.5 g (adult males). In practice, eating a variety of foods every day is all you need to do in order to ensure an adequate protein intake.

Deficiency of Proteins

Protein-calorie malnutrition (PCM) is the most prominent form of protein deficiency state. It is common among children during the first few years of life (i.e., between 1-3 years of age). PCM occurs primarily due to poverty, and infections like diarrhoea, respiratory infection, measles and intestinal worms. These infections increase the demand for calories and decrease the absorption and utilization of proteins. Clinically, PCM is manifested in two forms. These are: *Marasmus* and *Kwashikor*

(i) *Marasmus:* It is a clinical condition of protein energy malnutrition resulting from deficiency of total energy intake, usually occurs in the age-group of 1/2–5 years. It is characterized by severe muscle wasting, severe growth retardation, wasting of muscles, failure to gain weight, child feels good appetite but irritable, marked wasting of skin and bones, diarrhoea and modified hair texture.

(ii) *Kwashikor:* It results from consumption of adequate calories but a relative protein deficiency. Symptoms are mental changes, edema, anaemia, retarded growth, loss of appetite, diarrhoea, scanty hair growth.

Treatment of PCM

It can be treated by:

1. Giving adequate diet.
2. Treatment of infections and measures to prevent relapse.
3. Promoting health education.
4. Taking adequate care of the child's nutritional requirement.

Protein Deficiency in Adults

Reduced weight, anaemia, greater susceptibility to infection, frequent loose motions, lethargy, edema, delay in healing of wounds are common protein deficiency signs in adults.

FATS

Fats are concentrated sources of energy containing carbon, hydrogen and oxygen. They are derived from animal and vegetable sources. Animal sources include milk, cheese, butter, egg, meat, oily fish, while Vegetable oils, nuts etc. are some vegetable sources. Fats are classified under the following heads:

1. *Simple lipids*, e.g., triglyceride, waxes.

2. *Compound lipids*, e.g., phospholipids, glycolipids lipo-proteins.
3. *Derived lipids*, e.g., cholesterol. These are derivatives obtained from simple or compound lipids and still possess characteristics of lipids.

Fats are esters of glycerol with fatty acids. Fatty acids are classified into saturated and unsaturated fatty acids.

Saturated fatty acids, e.g., lauric acid, palmitic acid and stearic acid. These are mostly present in animal fat.

Unsaturated fatty acids, e.g., oleic acid, linoleic acid. These are mostly present in vegetable oils. Vanaspati contain high proportion of saturated fatty acids.

Linoleic is the most essential fatty acid. Essential fatty acids cannot be synthesized by human body and are derived from the food. The example of essential fatty acids (EFA) are linolenic acid, arachidonic acid. Essential fatty acids promote growth as well as maintain dermal integrity. Deficiency of EFA leads to some abnormal skin conditions.

Functions

The functions of fatty acids are:

1. They provide energy and heat.
2. They support certain organs of the body like kidneys, eyes.
3. Fatty acid transport fat soluble vitamin A, D, E, K.
4. They are helpful in storage of fat.

Fat is a concentrated source of energy.

Saturated Fat

Saturated fats include Hydrogenated Fats or Trans-Fats — frequently found in commercial bakery products and margarines. Saturated fat is generally solid at room temperature. It is found in animal meats, chicken skin, lard, butter, hard margarine, cheese, whole milk and anything these ingredients are used in, such as *cakes, chocolate, biscuits, pies* and *pastries*.

Non-Saturated Fat

Unsaturated fat (including monounsaturates and polyunsaturates) is usually liquid at room temperature and generally comes from *vegetable sources.*

The Best Fats/Oils

Really good fats/oils come from *unrefined* vegetable sources or oily fish. Here are some basic guidelines for how to choose the best type of fat.

- For cooking, choose extra virgin olive oil
- For salads, choose from flax oil, canola oil, soya oil, extra virgin olive oil, wheatgerm oil, walnut oil, hemp seed oil.
- Eat regular helpings of oily fish like salmon, mackerel, sardines, tuna.

Good Fats to Eat

Fat has an undeserved reputation as a diet food that is bad for weight loss and health. True, saturated fat is bad for health, as it is proven to clog arteries causing heart disease and stroke. However, health warnings to "avoid saturated fat" have been misinterpreted to mean "avoid ALL fats." But the truth is, good fat is absolutely essential for good health.

How Much Fat Do We Need in Our Daily Diet?

Official dietary health guidelines advise that fat makes up no more than 30 percent of total calories. On a 1600-calorie diet, this means about 50 grams of total fat per day. Of this, a maximum of 1/3 may be saturated fat.

VITAMINS

The name vitamin is obtained from "vital amines" as it was originally thought that these substances were all amines. Human body uses these substances to stay healthy and support its many functions. There are two types of vitamins: water-soluble and fat-soluble. The body needs vitamins to stay healthy and a varied diet usually gives you all the vitamins you need. Vitamins do not provide energy (calories) directly, but they do help regulate energy-producing processes. With the exception of vitamins D and K, vitamins cannot be synthesized by the human body and must be obtained from the diet. Vitamins have to come from food because they are not manufactured or formed by the body.

There are 13 essential vitamins and each one has a special role to play within the body, helping to regulate the processes such as cell growth and repair, reproduction and digestion. Vitamin B-6, Niacin, Natural Vitamin E and Zinc: Support sexual function in men. Vitamins are complex organic compounds required for vital metabolic functions in the body and are needed by the body in small quantities. They are grouped as :

1. *Fat soluble vitamins:* Vitamins A, D, E and K.
2. *Water soluble vitamins*: Vitamins B complex and C.

1. Vitamin A (RETINOL)

(i) *Source:* Milk, butter, ghee, egg, yolk, fish liver oils, green leafy vegetables, mango, orange, carrot, papaya, tomato.

(ii) *Daily requirement:* 750 mg (for adult), 250-600 mg (for children).

(iii) *Functions:* Vitamin A is essential for proper functioning of retina and vision. It also helps in the production of retinol pigments needed for vision in dim light. It is helpful to maintain functioning and integrity of glandular and epithelial tissues. It helps in skeletal growth and has an anti-infective action.

(iv) *Deficiency diseases:* Stunted growth, Night blindness – Inability to see in dim light, Keratinization, Xerophthalmia, Corneal Xerosis – Cornea of eye becomes dry, dull.

2. Vitamin B Complex

Vitamin B Complex is a water soluble vitamin. It consists of thiamin (B_1), riboflavin (B_2), pyridoxine (B_6), vitamin B_{12}, vitamin B_7, niacin, folic acid, and pantothenic acid.

3. Vitamin B_1 (Thiamine)

(i) *Source:* Unmilled cereals, pulses, oilseeds and nuts, rice polishings.

(ii) *Daily requirement:* Adult:1-1.5 mg.

(iii) *Functions:* It is required for proper utilization of carbohydrates in food, nutrition of nerve cells.

(iv) *Deficiency disease:* Loss of appetite, absence of ankle jerk or knee jerk and calf tenderness, ultimately leads to beri-beri.

4. Vitamin B_2 (Riboflavin)

(i) *Source:* Liver, yeast, milk, eggs, kidney and green leafy vegetables.

(ii) *Daily requirements:* Adult: 0.6 mg.

(iii) *Functions:* It acts as a coenzyme in the tissue oxidation and respiration. It is involved in the metabolism of carbohydrates, fats and proteins.

(iv) *Deficiency disease: Angular stomatitis* — Affection of the skin at the angles of mouth. *Cheilosis* — Zone of red, denuded epithelium appears at the line of closure of the lips. *Dermatitis, corneal vascularizaton* — Small greyish white opacities may be seen on the surface of cornea.

5. Pantothenic Acid (Vitamin B_3)

(i) *Source:* Liver, egg, meat, milk, yeast.

(ii) *Daily requirement:* Adult : 10 mg.

(iii) *Functions:* It is a component of coenzyme A involved in carbohydrate metabolism. It is required for synthesis of cholesterol and fatty acids. It is essential for biosynthesis of corticosteroids.

(iv) *Deficiency disease:* Burning-feet syndrome. (Itching and burning in the feet).

6. Vitamin B_6 (Pyridoxine, Pyridoxal and Pyridoxamine)

(i) *Source:* Vegetables (mainly legumes), bran of cereals, meat, egg yolk, pulses.

(ii) *Daily requirement:* Adult — 1-2 mg.

(iii) *Functions:* It is required for protein metabolism. It is essential for formation of RBC and WBC.

(iv) *Deficiency disease:* In infants — Convulsions. In adults — Dermatitis, glossitis, angular stomatitis.

7. Biotin (vitamin B_7 or Vitamin H)

(i) *Source:* Liver, egg yolk, yeast, pulses, nuts.

(ii) *Daily requirement:* Unknown.

(iii) *Function:* It is required in carbohydrate and fat metabolism.

(iv) *Deficiency disease:* Dermatitis. Conjunctivitis.

8. Vitamin B_{12} (Cyanacobalamin)

(i) *Source:* Liver, kidney, meat, fish, egg, cheese and fermenting liquors. In the human body, it is synthesized by the bacteria of colon.

(ii) *Daily requirement:* 1-15 mg. (Adult)

(iii) *Functions:* It is necessary for the maturation of RBCs in red bone marrow.

(iv) *Deficiency disease: Megaloblastic anaemia* — Deficiency of either vitamin B_6 or B_{12} results in megaloblastic anaemia due to faulty erythropoeisis and maturation of RBC. The bone marrow contains abnormal cells, called megaloblast in place of normoblast. *Pernicious anaemia* — Anaemia produced due to the deficiency of the intrinsic factor resulting in defective or decreased absorption of vitamin B_{12}. Degeneration of nerve fibre of spinal cord.

9. Vitamin C (Ascorbic Acid)

(i) *Source:* Citrus fruits and green leafy vegetables, Amla and Guava are the richest sources of ascorbic acid.

(ii) *Daily requirement:* Adult— 60 mg.

(iii) *Functions:* It has role in oxidative reaction in the tissue. It is needed for maintenance of the strength of the walls of the blood capillaries. It is required for development and maintenance of healthy bones and teeth. It is essential for formation of RBC. It facilitates Iron absorption by reducing ferric iron to ferrous form. It increases resistance of the body against infection.

(iv) *Deficiency disease:* Defective formation of collagen in connective tissues. Defective formation of bones and teeth. Capillary haemorrhage. Delayed healing of wounds. Anaemia. Gross deficiency causes Scurvy disease. It is characterized by gingivitis (inflammation of gums), cutaneous bleeding, Ecchymoses specially on the feet, delayed wound healing and anaemia.

10. Vitamin D

There are a number of closely related compound-sterols. All possess ricket preventing property. Out of these, two forms of vitamin D are important: Vit. D_1– Calciferol, Vit. D_2 – Chole calciferol.

(i) *Source :* Sunlight, milk, fish liver oils, cheese, egg, yolk and butter.

(ii) *Daily requirement:* Adult — 2.5 mg., Children — 5 mg.

(iii) *Function:* It facilitates the absorption and utilization of calcium and phosphorous for healthy bones and teeth.

(iv) *Deficiency disease: Rickets* — It is characterized by bone deformation in growing children. *Osteomalacia* — Generally found in pregnant, lactating mothers. It is a common metabolic disorder of bones and is characterized by chronic backache and generalised aches and pains.

11. Vitamin E (Tocopherols)

(i) *Source:* Vegetable oils, wheat germ oil, egg yolk, milk, green vegetables, nuts.

(ii) *Daily requirement:* Adult 8-10 mg.

(iii) *Function :* It maintains healthy muscular system and act as a anti-oxidant.

(iv) *Deficiency disease:* In human beings no ill effect due to deficiency has been reported.

12. Vitamin K (Phylloquinone)

(i) *Source:* Cabbage, cauliflower, fresh green vegetables, fruits, fish liver.

(ii) *Daily requirement:* 70-140 gm.

(iii) *Functions:* It is essential for the formation of prothrombin in liver. Prothrombin is a second clotting factor. It is essential for the formation of clotting factors VII, IX and X in liver.

(iv) *Deficiency diseases:* Promotion content is reduced and blood clotting time is prolonged.

13. Vitamin M (Folic Acid)

(i) *Source:* Green leafy vegetables, liver, egg, yeast, milk, fruits and cereals.

(ii) *Daily requirement:* Adult: 100 mg per day.

(iii) *Function*: It is needed for the formation of RBC.

(iv) *Deficiency disease:* Megaloblastic anaemia, Glossitis, Disturbances of GIT like diarrhoea, distension and flatulence, Severe deficiency may cause infertility or sterility.

14. Nicotonic Acid (NIACIN)

(i) *Source* : Liver, groundnut, cereals, pulses, meat, fish.

(ii) *Daily requirement:* Unknown.

(iii) *Functions:* It serves as a component of coenzymes which are essential for the metabolism of carbohydrates, fats and proteins. It is needed for normal functioning of skin and nervous system.

(iv) *Deficiency disease* : Dermatitis, diarrhoea, dementia.

TRACE ELEMENTS

Trace elements are the minerals that the human body needs in minute amounts, 15 mg/day or less. Some of the important ones are discussed below:

1. Iodine

Sea foods and vegetables grown on iodine-rich soils are good sources of iodine. Milk and egg from animals and poultry fed on iodine-containing diets also furnish iodine.

An adult man requires 0.15 mg and an adult woman 0.1 mg of iodine every day. Pregnant and lactating women need vitamins as much. A pinhead of iodine suffices for a month; and a teaspoonful, for life.

Iodine is necessary for the formation of thyroxin and triiodothyronine, which are essential for the normal metabolism of many cells. The thyroid hormones control protein synthesis, regulate calcium metabolism and inhibit release of thyrotropin from the pituitary.

2. Copper

Cereals, pulses, nuts and liver are good sources of copper. The daily requirement of copper is 2-3 mg. Copper helps in iron utilization and RBC production. Along with vitamin C, it helps the formation of elastin, an essential component of muscle fiber. Also, copper promotes bone formation. Deficiency of copper gives rise to weakness, skin ulceration, anemia and neutropenia.

3. Zinc

Cereals, pulses, nuts, milk, meat, fish, oyster and herring are good sources of zinc. The daily requirement is 15 mg. Zinc is needed for protein synthesis, phosphorous metabolism, the development of reproductive organs, male hormone production and wound healing. Also, it maintains body's alkaline-acid balance. Zinc is a component of superoxide dismutase, an enzyme that scavenges free radicals. Zinc deficiency is associated with hypogeusia (loss or perversion of the taste sensation), physical underdevelopment, delayed sexual maturity, fatigue, decreased alertness, and white spots on finger nails.

4. Cobalt

Cobalt is widely distributed in foods. It is an important constituent of vitamin B_{12}. It helps in transporting glucose from blood to cells. It is necessary for the repair of myelin sheath. Cobalt deficiency gives rise to increased susceptibility to inter-current infections, anemia, retarded physical development, digestive disturbances and nerve damage.

5. Chromium

Chromium aids insulin in maintaining blood glucose level. It helps with amino acid transportation in the body and reduces cholesterol and triglyceride levels. Deficiency of chromium gives rise to tiredness, obesity, heart disease and cancers.

6. Manganese

Manganese is needed for the metabolism of thiamine and vitamin E, and the production of sex hormones. It catalyses digestive enzymes. Being a component of superoxide dismutase, it has anti-oxidant properties. Deficiency of manganese is associated with digestive problems, loss of hearing, ataxia, convulsions and paralysis.

7. Selenium

Plant foods, meat, and sea foods contain selenium. Its daily requirement is 55 mg. Selenium is necessary for the normal functioning of thyroid and the immune system of the body. Selenium is an antioxidant and prevents generation of free radicals. Thus it slows down ageing, and reduces the risk of cancer and chronic diseases of heart and blood vessels. Selenium deficiency gives rise to dandruff, premature ageing, heart disease and cancers, particularly of lungs, colon and rectum. Two rare diseases of infancy and young childhood due to selenium deficiency are cardiomyopathy (Keshan disease) and osteoarthritis (Kashin-Beck disease).

8. Magnesium

This element assists calcium and vitamin C metabolism. It helps in the release of energy from sugars. Also, it controls neuromuscular activity of heart. It is a general anti-oxidant. Magnesium deficiency is characterized by heightened muscular excitability, nervousness and confusion. Chronic deficiency of magnesium increases the risk of renal stone formation.

9. Molybdenum

Beans, dark green vegetables and grains contain molybdenum. The daily requirement of this element is 75-250 mg. Molybdenum is needed for metabolism of iron, detoxification of sulfates and the conversion of purine into uric acid. Molybdenum deficiency causes brain damage in early infancy and, in later life, cancers of, specially, mouth and esophagus.

10. Other Trace Elements

Some of the other trace elements are fluorine, bromine, nickel, and boron.

FOOD ADDITIVES

Food additives are the legally permitted substances added to food to improve its appearance, flavor, colour, nutritive value or storage property. The term refers also to the non-nutritive substances that get incorporated into foods in the course of their packaging, storage, transportation and handling. The addition of substances not legally permitted or deliberate addition of substances for dishonest commercial gain is food adulteration. Such substances therefore are called food adulterants. There are two kinds of food additives:

1. Direct or first category additives. These are the substances deliberately added.
2. Indirect or second category additives. These find their way to food during its handling, packaging, transportation, etc. Examples are DOT, BHC, rodenticides, arsenic, lead, etc.

Following are the harmful effects of food additives:

1. Tartrazine gives rise, in the susceptible individuals, to asthma, rashes and migraine.
2. DOT, BHC, arsenic and lead give rise to poisoning.
3. Nitrites give rise to nitrosamine, which is a carcinogen.
4. Benzoic acid causes neurological symptoms.
5. Monosodium glutamate produces dizziness, burning sensations and chest tightness.
6. Rhodamine is responsible for tumors of lung, breast and ovary.

FOOD ADULTERANTS

Food adulterants are of two kinds: (a) worthless, inferior or spurious substances that are added to foods by unscrupulous traders and (b) the prohibited additives. Some examples of adulterants and the foods to which they are added follow:

(i) *Worthless substances:* Stone chips and chaff are added to cereals. Cow dung powder and wood shavings are mixed with turmeric powder and chilli powder, respectively. Chalk powder is added to milk. Blotting paper is mixed with ice cream. Used tea leaf is combined with fresh tea leaf.

(ii) *Inferior matter mixed with superior one and sold as wholly superior food:* Discoloured and fungus-spoiled rice with healthy rice; vanaspati with ghee; jaggery solution with honey; and crude oil with edible oil.

(iii) *Spurious matter passed off as genuine food:* Tamarind seeds are sold as coffee beans. Papaya seeds are sold as black pepper. Prohibited additives are—lead chromate, metanil yellow, ferric sulfate, and copper carbonate.

(iv) *Food adulteration:* Legally food adulteration is much broader in scope than the addition of worthless, spurious, and inferior substances or of prohibited additives. Apart from addition it includes the following:

   (a) *Dilution:* Addition of water to milk is adulteration.

   (b) *Abstraction:* Removal of cream from milk is an example of adulteration by abstraction.

   (c) *Substitution:* An example is the substitution of starch for fat in diluted milk in order to increase its specific gravity.

   (d) *Mislabelling:* Affixing the label of 'pure coffee' on the bottle filled with a mixture of coffee and chicory is adulteration.

   (e) *Putting up for sale stale food as fresh one:* The selling of old meat brightened with red dye as fresh meat constitutes the offense of adulteration.

(v) *Selling of prohibited item:* Selling of non-iodized salt is adulteration.

Following are the hazards of food adulteration: Epidemic dropsy, poisoning from lead chromate, dyes, etc., gastritis (from the ingestion of copper bicarbonate). and testicular damage (from metanil yellow).

For preventing adulteration an Act called the *Prevention of Food Adulteration Act* was passed in 1954. Standards for different foods have been laid down in this Act. Food inspectors employed by local authorities visit shops, take samples of suspected foods and send them for analysis. If the adulteration is proved the trader is awarded a punishment of 6 months imprisonment and a fine ranging from 1,000 to 5,000 rupees.

FUNCTIONS OF FOOD

1. Growth and Repair

Foods provide the raw materials for the growth of the body (from the birth weight and height of about 2.8 kg and 48 cm to the adult measurements of 55 kg and 165 cm, respectively). Also they provide substance for the replacement of dead tissue (as cells constantly die and are replaced by new ones).

Foods that principally serve this function are called the body building foods. These are the ones that are rich in high-class proteins such as milk, egg, meat, fish, etc.

2. Regulation of Vital Processes

Following are some of the functions for which foods are required:

(i) The synthesis of hormones (such as insulin and thyroxin), pigments (haemoglobin, rhodopsin), enzymes (carboxylase, cytochrome oxidase, coenzyme A), biological lubricants (saliva, synovial fluid), plasma proteins and mucopoly-saccharides.

(ii) The coagulation of blood.

(iii) The contraction of muscles including cardiac muscle.

(iv) The transport of oxygen in the blood.

(v) The regulation of heart beats.

(vi) The maintenance of the osmotic pressure.

(vii) The stimulation of the intestinal motility.

3. Supply of Energy

Energy is needed by the human body for the following purposes:

(i) Regulation of temperature of the body.

(ii) Elimination of the products of excretion.

(iii) Absorption and digestion of foods.

(iv) Physical activities.

(v) The beating of heart and the contraction of the respiratory muscles.

MINERALS

Minerals are inorganic compounds necessary for the growth of vital body-functions and for repair of tissues. They are broadly classified in two groups :

1. *Major minerals:* For example, calcium, iron, phosphorous, sodium, potassium, magnesium.
2. *Trace elements:* Required in small quantity by the body, e.g., iron, iodine, fluorine, zinc, copper, cobalt, chromium, manganese etc.

1. Calcium

(i) *Source:* Milk, cheese, eggs, green vegetables, fish.

(ii) *Daily requirement:* 400-500 mg (Adult). 1000 mg/day (Pregnancy and lactation). 500-600 mg (Children).

(iii) *Functions:* It is required for hardening of bone and teeth, coagulation of blood, muscle contraction, activation of some important enzyme reactions in body.

2. Phosphorous

(i) *Source*: Cereals, pulses, nuts, oilseeds, cheese, meat, liver.

(ii) *Functions*: It is associated with calcium and vitamin D in the hardening of bones and teeth. It maintains the constant composition of body fluids.

3. Sodium

(i) *Source:* Most of the foods especially fish, meat, egg, milk, artificially enriched bread, cooking and table salt.

(ii) *Daily requirement:* 2-5 gm.

(iii) *Functions:* It is required for contraction of muscle, transmission of nerve impulse in nerve fibres, maintenance of electolyte balance in the body.

4. Potassium

(i) *Source:* Widely distributed in all foods.

(ii) *Daily requirement:* 5-7 gm.

(iii) *Functions:* It is essential for contraction of muscles, transmission of nerve impulse, maintenance of electolyte balance in the body.

5. Fluorine

(i) *Source:* Drinking water, sea fish and tea.

(ii) *Daily requirement:* Optimum level of fluoride in drinking water is 0.5 - 0.8 mg/litre.

(iii) *Functions:* It is essential for the normal mineralization of bones and formation of dental enamel. Ingestion of large quantities causes — dental and skeletal fluorosis.

(iv) *Deficiency disease:* It is characterised by dental caries, which can be prevented by fluoridation of community water supplies.

6. Zinc

(i) *Source:* Zinc is widely distributed in foodstuffs, both animal and vegetable. It is constituent of insulin and many enzymes.

(ii) *Daily requirement:* 12 mg.

(iii) *Deficiency disease:* It is associated with liver disease, pernicious anaemia, delayed wound healing, sexual dysfunction and alopecia.

7. Iron

(i) *Source*: Liver, meat, kidney, egg yolk, cereals, pulses, green leafy vegetable, legumes. Significant quantity of iron can be derived from cooking in iron utensils.

(ii) *Daily requirements:* 24 – 30 mg daily. However requirement is increased upto 60 mg during growth, menstruation, pregnancy and lactation.

(iii) *Functions*: Iron is required for the formation of haemoglobin in RBC, myoglobin. It is essential for cell respiration, transport of oxygen and tissue oxidation. It is required for brain development and muscle activity. It is required for the regulation of body temperature and for the metabolism of catecholamines. It is also required for the maintenance of immune system.

(iv) *Deficiency disease:* Leads to anaemia, impaired immunity and decreased resistance to infection.

8. Iodine

(i) *Source:* Sea fish, shell fish, iodized salt, vegetables grown in soil containing iodine.

(ii) *Daily requirement:* 100–200 p.g.

(iii) *Function:* It is required for formation of thyroxine, tri-iodothyronine the hormones secreted by the thyroid gland, Iodine deficiency leads to endemicgoitre, hypothyroidism, impaired hearing and brain development, spontaneous abortions.

WATER

Water is the most important nutrient because the functions of cells depend on a fluid environment. Water composes 60 percent to 70 percent of total body weight. Lean people's bodies contains more water than obese people's bodies. Infants have the greatest percentage of total body weight as water and older people have the least. As a result, they are most vulnerable to water deprivation or loss. Yet, no one, when deprived of water, can survive more than a few hours in a desert or a few days in the most protective environment. Fluid needs are met by consumption of liquids and a solid foods such as fresh fruits and vegetables, and water is produced when food is oxidized during digestion. In healthy individual the fluid intake from all sources equals the fluid output through elimination, respiration, and sweating. An ill person can have an increased need for fluid (e.g., fever). An ill person can also have a decreased need for fluid (e.g., cardio-pulmonary or renal disease).

MALNUTRITION

Malnutrition implies the result of imperfect assimilation nutrition or both. It has been defined as a pathological state resulting from a relative or absolute deficiency or excess of one or more essential nutrients.

TYPES OF MALNUTRITION

Malnutrition may be in the following forms:

(i) *Undernutrition:* It is due to insufficient food eaten over an extended period of time due to poverty or ignorance.

(ii) *Overnutrition:* It is due to consumption of excessive quantity of food over an extended period of time due to excessive food or ignorance.

(iii) *Imbalance:* It is due to imbalance such as quantitative imbalance of calcium, phosphorus and vitamin D.

(iv) *Specific deficiency:* It is due to specific deficiency such as goitre in iodine deficiency.

Malnutrition is a condition that is most prevalent in our country. It is more common among children, pregnant ladies and nursing mothers. Its effects are kwashiokor, marasmus, xerophthalmia, beri beri, pellagra, goitre, rickets, etc. This malnutrition condition predisposes to diseases like tuberculosis, diarrhea, parasitic infestation leads to high sickness rate and increased infant mortality rate.

CAUSES FOR MALNUTRITION IN INDIA

(i) *Population growth:* The rapid growth of population leads to gap between food production and food consumption which causes malnutrition.

(ii) *Agriculture and food production:* In India food production depends upon nature. There is no proper adequate source of timely irrigation. Farmers have to depend on natural rainfall, which is unpredictable. At one time unprecedented drought is followed by flood at another time. Fragmentation of land and bad socio-economic conditions are also responsible.

(iii) *Prevalence of parasitic and infectious diseases:* These diseases are responsible for decreased intestinal absorption and lack of proper work which is important for poor and inadequate diet.

(iv) *Religious and cultural food fads:* These prevent the people from using the locally available nutritious food. Cooking methods also differ according to tradition.

(v) *General illiteracy and ignorance:* These are responsible about the importance of balanced diet and poverty.

(vi) *Economic barrier:* It has also resulted in malnutrition among the children of the nation.

PREVENTIVE MEASURES OF MALNUTRITION

1. Increased food production by scientific cultivation.
2. Vulnerable group, i.e., infants, pre-school children, expectant and lactating mothers should be protected by best utilization of locally available food substitution, midday cheap supplementary food, etc.
3. Fortification of *atta* (flour). Flour should be fortified with vitamin A and vitamin D.
4. Improvement of environmental sanitation is necessary to prevent the parasitic infections.
5. Projects and programme in the field of food and nutrition including nutrition education should receive a high priority.
6. Applied nutrition programme should be extended to all the affected areas and it should run sincerely and should be beneficial to vulnerable groups.
7. Prevention of unnecessary loss of food in the fields, store, transport and cooking is necessary.
8. Education of public on fundamentals of diet and nutrition and help from voluntary and international organizations is necessary.

Malnutrition is a disease of society, poverty and ignorance. In this, every one, i.e. teacher, nurse, physician, farmer and all organizations have to contribute much to combat this malnutrition. The steps have already been taken by the Government of India to tackle the problem.

STUDY QUESTIONS

1. Discuss in brief high risk strategy in vitamin A deficiency.
2. Write short notes on the following:
   (a) Vitamin B complex;
   (b) Vitamin C; and
   (c) Vitamin D.
3. Enumerate the Fat soluble vitamins. Give the detail about the functions, sources and deficiency of Vitamin D.
4. Explain the meaning of Malnutrition.

4

Demography and Family Planning

DEMOGRAPHY

Demography is the statistical study of all populations. It can be a very general science that can be applied to any kind of dynamic population, that is, one that changes over time or space. It encompasses the study of the size, structure and distribution of populations, and spatial and/or temporal changes in them in response to birth, migration, aging and death.

Demographic analysis can be applied to whole societies or to groups defined by criteria such as education, nationality, religion and ethnicity. In academia, demography is often regarded as a branch of either anthropology, economics, or sociology. Formal demography limits its object of study to the measurement of population processes, while the more broad field of social demography population studies also analyze the relationships between economic, social, cultural and biological processes influencing a population.

DATA AND METHODS

There are two methods of data collection: *direct* and *indirect*. ***Direct data*** come from vital statistics registries that track all births and deaths as well as certain changes in legal status such as marriage, divorce, and migration (registration of place of residence). In developed countries with good registration systems, registry statistics are the best method for estimating the number of births and deaths.

The *census* is the other common *direct method* of collecting demographic data. A census is usually conducted by a national government and attempts to enumerate every person in a country. However, in contrast to vital statistics data, which are typically collected continuously and summarized on an annual basis, censuses typically occur only every 10 years or so, and thus are not usually the best source of data on births and deaths. Analyses are conducted after a census to estimate how much over- or undercounting took place. Censuses do more than just count people. They typically collect information about families or households, as well as about such individual characteristics as age, sex, marital status, literacy/education, employment status and occupation, and geographical location.

They may also collect data on migration (or place of birth or of previous residence), language, religion, nationality (or ethnicity or race), and citizenship. In countries in which the vital registration system may be incomplete, the censuses are also used as a direct source of information about fertility and mortality.

Indirect methods of data collections are required in countries where full data are not available, such as is the case in much of the developing world. One of these techniques is the sister method, where survey researchers ask women how many of their sisters have died or had children and at what age. With these surveys, researchers can then indirectly estimate birth or death rates for the entire population. Other indirect methods include asking people about siblings, parents, and children.

INDICATORS OF DEMOGRAPHY

Important indicators in demography include:

- The *crude birth rate,* the annual number of live births per 1000 people.

- The *general fertility rate,* the annual number of live births per 1000 women of child-bearing age (often taken to be from 15 to 49 years old, but sometimes from 15 to 44).
- *Age-specific fertility rates,* the annual number of live births per 1000 women in particular age-groups (usually age 15-19, 20-24 etc.)
- The *crude death rate,* the annual number of deaths per 1000 people.
- The *infant mortality rate,* the annual number of deaths of children less than 1-year old per 1000 live births.
- The *expectation of life* (or life-expectancy), the number of years which an individual at a given age could expect to live at present mortality levels.
- The *total fertility rate,* the number of live births per woman completing her reproductive life, if her child-bearing at each age reflected current age-specific fertility rates.
- The *gross reproduction rate,* the number of daughters who would be born to a woman completing her reproductive life at current age-specific fertility rates.
- The *net reproduction ratio* is the expected number of daughters, per newborn prospective mother, who may or may not survive to and through the ages of child-bearing.

Note that the crude death rate as defined above and applied to a whole population can give a misleading impression. For example, the number of deaths per 1000 people can be higher for developed nations than in less-developed countries, despite standards of health being better in developed countries. This is because developed countries have relatively more older people, who are more likely to die in a given year, so that the overall mortality rate can be higher even if the mortality rate at any given age is lower. A more complete picture of mortality is given by a life table which summarises mortality separately at each age. A life-table is necessary to give a good estimate of life-expectancy.

The fertility rates can also give a misleading impression that a population is growing faster than it in fact is, because measurement of fertility rates only involves the reproductive rate of women, and does not adjust for the sex ratio. For example, if a population has a total fertility rate of 4.0 but the sex ratio is 66/34 (twice as many men as women), this population is actually growing at a slower natural increase rate than would a population having a fertility rate of 3.0 and a sex ratio of 50/50.

FERTILITY

Fertility is the natural capability of giving life. As a measure, "Fertility Rate" is the number of children born per couple, person or population. This is different from fecundity, which is defined as the potential for reproduction (influenced by gamete production, fertilisation and carrying a pregnancy to term). In the English language, the term was originally applied only to females, but increasingly is applied to males as well, as common understanding of reproductive mechanisms increases and the importance of the male role is better known. Infertility is a deficient fertility.

Human fertility depends on factors of nutrition, sexual behavior, culture, instinct, endocrinology, timing, economics, way of life, and emotions. Animal fertility is no less complex.

THE DEMOGRAPHY OF FERTILITY

The level of fertility in the world varies broadly by country and culture, social and economic conditions, as well as by individual characteristics such as age. Generally, more industrialized and economically developed societies have lower fertility than agricultural and less developed societies. Also, within countries, generally, more educated groups with higher incomes have lower fertility than less educated groups with lower incomes. Historically, as groups within countries have improved their living standards, and nations have become more economically developed, health conditions have improved, morbidity and mortality have declined, and fertility has declined due to the adoption of fertility-constraining behaviours, such as the limitation of sexual relations or marriage, practice of contraception, and resort to induced abortion. This sequence of events has been observed in western industrialized societies over the last two centuries, and in developing regions in the last half century. The process is often referred to as the demographic transition, and it comprises the principal theoretical base for research conducted by demographers, sociologists, anthropologists, epidemiologists, economists, and others, on the determinants and consequences of the levels of mortality and fertility of national and regional populations.

FAMILY PLANNING

Family planning is frequently used to mean that people plan when to have children, using birth control and other techniques to implement that plan. Other techniques commonly used include sexuality education, prevention and management of sexually transmitted infections, preconceptional counselling and management, and infertility management. Family planning is sometimes used as a synonym for the use of birth control, though it often includes more.

It is most usually applied to the circumstance of a monogamous female-male couple who wish to limit the number of children they have and/or to control the timing of pregnancy (also known as spacing children).

Waiting until mother is at least 18 years old before trying to have children improves maternal and child health. If additional children are desired, it is healthier for both the mother and child to wait at least 2 years after the previous birth before attempting to conceive (but not more than 5 years). After a miscarriage or abortion, it is healthier to wait at least 6 months.

CONTRACEPTIVE METHODS OF FAMILY PLANNING

Birth control, sometimes synonymous with contraception, is a regimen of one or more actions, devices, or medications followed in order to deliberately prevent or reduce the likelihood of pregnancy or childbirth. "Contraception" may refer specifically to mechanisms that are intended to reduce the likelihood of a sperm cell fertilizing the egg. Birth control is commonly used as part of family planning.

Physical Methods

Physical methods may work in a variety of ways, among them: physically preventing sperm from entering the female reproductive tract; hormonally preventing ovulation from occurring; making the woman's reproductive tract inhospitable to sperm; or surgically altering the male or female reproductive tract to induce sterility. Some methods use more than one mechanism. Physical methods vary in simplicity, convenience and efficacy.

Barrier Methods

Barrier methods place a physical impediment to the movement of sperm into the female reproductive tract.

The most popular barrier method is the ***male condom,*** a latex or polyurethane sheath placed over the penis. The condom is also available in a female version, which is made of polyurethane. The female condom has a flexible ring at each end — one secures behind the pubic bone to hold the condom in place, while the other ring stays outside the vagina.

Cervical barriers are devices that are contained completely within the vagina. The contraceptive sponge has a depression to hold it in place over the cervix. The cervical cap is the smallest cervical barrier. Depending on the type of cap, it stays in place by suction to the cervix or to the vaginal walls. The diaphragm fits into place behind the woman's pubic bone and has a firm but flexible ring, which helps it press against the vaginal walls.

Spermicide may be placed in the vagina before intercourse and creates a chemical barrier. Spermicide may be used alone, or in combination with a physical barrier.

Hormonal Methods

Ortho Tri-cyclen, a brand of oral contraceptive, in a dial dispenser. There are a variety of delivery methods for hormonal contraception.

Combinations of synthetic oestrogens and progestins (synthetic progestogens) are commonly used. These include the combined oral contraceptive pill ("The Pill"), the Patch, and the contraceptive vaginal ring ("NuvaRing").

Other methods contain only a *progestin* (a synthetic progestogen). These include the 'progesterone only pill' (the POP or "minipill"), the injectables Depo Provera (a depot formulation of medroxyprogesterone acetate given as an intramuscular injection every three months) and Noristerat (Norethindrone acetate given as an intramuscular injection every 8 weeks), and contraceptive implants. The 'progestin-only pill' must be taken at more precisely remembered times each day than combined pills.

Intrauterine Methods

Intrauterine devices are devices which are placed inside the uterus. They are usually shaped like a "T" — the arms of the T hold the device in place. There are two main types of intrauterine contraceptives: those that contain copper (which has a spermicidal effect), and those that release a progestogen.

Induced Abortion

Abortion can be done with surgical methods, usually suction-aspiration abortion (in the first trimester) or dilation and evacuation (in the second trimester). Medical abortion uses drugs to end a pregnancy and is approved for pregnancies where the length of gestation has not exceeded 8 weeks. Some herbs are believed to cause abortion (abortifacients). The efficacy of these plants as such has never been studied in humans.

Sterilization

Surgical sterilization is available in the form of tubal ligation for women and vasectomy for men. In women, the process may be referred to as "tying the tubes," but the fallopian tubes may be tied, cut, clamped, or blocked. This serves to prevent sperm from joining the unfertilized egg. The non-surgical sterilization procedure, Essure, is an example of a procedure that blocks the tubes. Sterilization should be considered permanent.

Behavioural Methods

Behavioural methods involve regulating the timing or methods of intercourse to prevent the introduction of sperm into the female reproductive tract, either altogether or when an egg may be present.

Fertility Awareness

Symptoms-based methods of fertility awareness involve a woman's observation and charting of her body's fertility signs, to determine the fertile and infertile phases of her cycle. Charting may be done by hand or with the assistance of software. Most methods track one or more of the three primary fertility signs: changes in basal body temperature, in cervical mucus, and in cervical position. If a woman tracks both basal body temperature and another primary sign, the method is referred to as symptothermal. Other bodily cues such as mittelschmerz are considered secondary indicators.

Fertility monitors are computerized devices that determine fertility or infertility based on, for example, temperature or urinalysis tests. Calendar-based methods such as the rhythm method and Standard Days Method estimate the likelihood of fertility based on the length of past menstrual cycles. To avoid pregnancy with fertility awareness, unprotected sex is restricted to the least fertile period. During the most fertile period, barrier methods may be availed, or she may abstain from intercourse.

The term natural family planning (NFP) is sometimes used to refer to any use of FA methods. However, this term specifically refers to the practices which are permitted by the Roman Catholic Church — breastfeeding infertility, and periodic abstinence during fertile times. FA methods may be used by NFP users to identify these fertile times.

Coitus Interruptus

Coitus interruptus (literally "interrupted sex"), also known as the withdrawal method, is the practice of ending sexual intercourse ("pulling out") before ejaculation. The main risk of coitus interruptus is that the man may not perform the manocuvre correctly, or may not perform the manocuvre in a timely manner. Although concern has been raised about the risk of pregnancy from sperm in pre-ejaculate, several small studies have failed to find any viable sperm in the fluid.

Avoiding Vaginal Intercourse

The risk of pregnancy from non-vaginal sex, such as outercourse (sex without penetration), anal sex, or oral sex is virtually zero. (A very small risk comes from the possibility of semen leaking onto the vulva (with anal sex) or coming into contact with an object, such as a hand, that later contacts the vulva.)

Abstinence

Sexual abstinence is the practice of refraining from all sexual activity.

Lactational

Most breastfeeding women have a period of infertility after the birth of their child. The lactational amenorrhea method, or LAM, gives guidelines for determining the length of a woman's period of breastfeeding infertility.

PHYSICAL BARRIER OF CONTRACEPTIVE

The only forms of contraceptives currently available to men are condoms, the withdrawal method, and vasectomy. Other forms of male contraception are in various stages of research and development.

CONDOM

Condom is a device most commonly used during sexual intercourse. It is put on a man's erect penis and physically blocks ejaculated semen from entering the body of a sexual partner. Condoms are used to prevent pregnancy and transmission of sexually transmitted diseases (STDs—such as gonorrhea, syphilis, and HIV). Because condoms are waterproof, elastic, and durable, they are also used in a variety of secondary applications. These range from creating waterproof microphones to protecting rifle barrels from clogging.

In the modern age, condoms are most often made from latex, but some are made from other materials such as polyurathane, or lamb intestine. A female condom is also available, most often made of polyurathane. As a method of contraception, male condoms have the advantage of being inexpensive, easy to use, having few side-effects, and of offering protection against sexually transmitted diseases. With proper knowledge and application technique—and use at every act of intercourse—users of male condoms experience a 2% per-year pregnancy rate.

VARIETIES

Most condoms have a reservoir tip or teat end, making it easier to accommodate the man's ejaculate. Condoms come in different sizes, from oversized to snug and they also come in a variety of surfaces intended to stimulate the user's partner. Condoms are usually supplied with a lubricant coating to facilitate penetration, while flavoured condoms are principally used for oral sex. As mentioned above, most condoms are made of latex, but polyurethane and lambskin condoms are also widely available.

MATERIALS

Natural Latex

An unrolled latex condom Latex has outstanding elastic properties: Its tensile strength exceeds 30 MPa, and latex condoms may be stretched in excess of 800% before breaking. Every latex

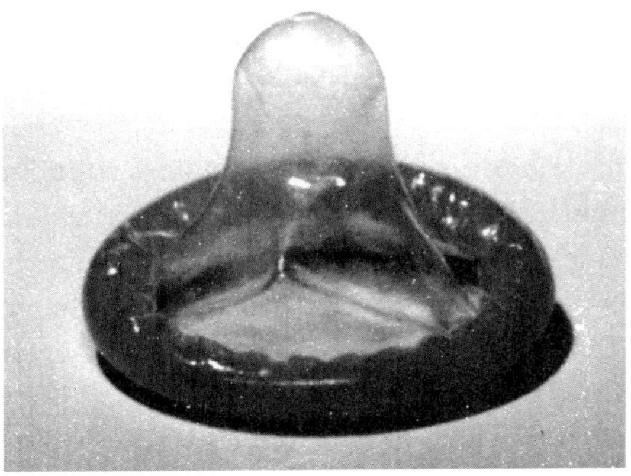

Fig. 4.1 *Condom.*

condom is tested for holes with an electrical current. If the condom passes, it is rolled and packaged. In addition, a portion of each batch of condoms is subject to water leak and air burst testing. Latex condoms used with oil-based lubricants (e.g., vaseline) are likely to break or slip off due to loss of elasticity caused by the oils.

Synthetic

The most common non-latex condoms are made from polyurethane. Condoms may also be made from other synthetic materials, such as AT-10 resin, and most recently polyisoprene.

Polyurethane condoms tend to be the same width and thickness as latex condoms, with most polyurethane condoms between 0.04 mm and 0.07 mm thick. Polyurethane is also the material of many female condoms.

Polyurethane can be considered better than latex in several ways: it conducts heat better than latex, is not as sensitive to temperature and ultraviolet light (and so has less rigid storage requirements and a longer shelf life), can be used with oil-based lubricants, is less allergenic than latex, and does not have an odor.

However, polyurethane condoms are less elastic than latex ones, and may be more likely to slip or break than latex, and are more expensive. Polyisoprene is a synthetic version of natural rubber latex. While significantly more expensive, it has the advantages of latex (such as being softer and more elastic than polyurethane condoms) without the protein which is responsible for latex allergies.

Lambskin

Condoms made from one of the oldest condom materials, labelled "lambskin" (made from lamb intestines) are still available. They have a greater ability to transmit body warmth and tactile sensation, when compared to synthetic condoms, and are less allergenic than latex. However, there is an increased risk of transmitting STDs compared to latex because of pores in the material, which are thought to be large enough to allow infectious agents to pass through, *albeit* blocking the passage of sperm.

Lambskin condoms are also significantly more expensive than other types.

Spermicidal

Some latex condoms are lubricated at the manufacturer with a small amount of a non-oxynol-9, a spermicidal chemical. According to Consumer Reports, spermicidally lubricated condoms have no additional benefit in preventing pregnancy, have a shorter shelf life, and may cause urinary-tract infections in women. In contrast, application of separately packaged spermicide is believed to increase the contraceptive efficacy of condoms.

Non-oxynol-9 was once believed to offer additional protection against STDs (including HIV) but recent studies have shown that, with frequent use, non-oxynol-9 may increase the risk of HIV transmission. The World Health Organization says that spermicidally lubricated condoms should no longer be promoted. However, they recommend using a non-oxynol-9 lubricated condom over no condom at all.

EFFECTIVENESS

In Preventing Pregnancy

The effectiveness of condoms, as of most forms of contraception, can be assessed two ways. Perfect use or method effectiveness rates only include people who use condoms properly and consistently. Actual use, or typical use effectiveness rates are of all condom users, including those who use condoms improperly, inconsistently, or both. Rates are generally presented for the first year of use.

In Preventing STDs

Condoms are widely recommended for the prevention of sexually transmitted diseases (STDs). They have been shown to be effective in reducing infection rates in both men and women. While not perfect, the condom is effective at reducing the transmission of HIV, genital herpes, genital warts, syphilis, chlamydia, gonorrhea, and other diseases.

Although a condom is effective in limiting exposure, some disease transmission may occur even with a condom. Infectious areas of the genitals, especially when symptoms are present, may not be covered by a condom, and as a result, some diseases can be transmitted by direct contact.The primary effectiveness issue with using condoms to prevent STDs, however, is inconsistent use.

Condoms may also be useful in treating potentially *pre-cancerous cervical changes*. Exposure to human papillomavirus, even in individuals already infected with the virus, appears to increase the risk of precancerous changes. The use of condoms helps promote regression of these changes.

CAUSES OF FAILURE

Barrier Birth Control and Spermicide Condoms may slip off the penis after ejaculation, break due to improper application or physical damage (such as tears caused when opening the package), or break or slip due to latex degradation (typically from usage past the expiration date, improper storage, or exposure to oils). The rate of breakage is between 0.4% and 2.3%, while the rate of slippage is between 0.6% and 1.3%. Even if no breakage or slippage is observed, 1–2% of women will test positive for semen residue after intercourse with a condom. "Double bagging," using two condoms at once, also increases the risk of condom failure.

Different modes of condom failure result in different levels of semen exposure. If a failure occurs during application, the damaged condom may be disposed of and a new condom applied before intercourse begins – such failures generally pose no risk to the user.

Standard condoms will fit almost any penis, although many condom manufacturers offer "snug" or "magnum" sizes. Some manufacturers also offer custom sized-to-fit condoms, with claims that they are more reliable and offer improved sensation/comfort.

Experienced condom users are significantly less likely to have a condom slip or break compared to first-time users, although users who experience one slippage or breakage are more likely to suffer a second such failure.

Among people who intend condoms to be their form of birth control, pregnancy may occur when the user has sex without a condom. The person may have run out of condoms, or be travelling and not have a condom with thin, or simply dislike the feel of condoms and decide to "take a chance." This type of behaviour is the primary cause of typical use failure (as opposed to method or perfect use failure).

Another possible cause of condom failure is sabotage. One motive is to have a child against a partner's wishes or consent. Some commercial sex workers report clients sabotaging condoms in retaliation for being coerced into condom use. Placing pinholes in the tip of the condom is believed to significantly impact their effectiveness.

DIAPHRAGM

The diaphragm is a cervical barrier type of birth control. It is a soft latex or silicone dome with a spring moulded into the rim. The spring creates a seal against the walls of the vagina.

Anyone inserting or removing a diaphragm should first wash their hands, to avoid introducing harmful bacteria into the vaginal canal.

The rim of a diaphragm is squeezed into an oval or arc shape for insertion. A water-based lubricant (usually spermicide) may be applied to the rim of the diaphragm to aid insertion. One teaspoon (5 ml) of spermicide may be placed in the dome of the diaphragm before insertion, or with an applicator after insertion.

Diaphragms come in different sizes. A fitting appointment with a healthcare professional is necessary to determine which size a woman should wear.

A correctly fitting diaphragm will cover the cervix and rest snugly against the pubic bone. A diaphragm that is too small might fit inside the vagina without covering the cervix, or might become dislodged from the cervix during intercourse or bowel movements. It is also more likely, during intercourse, that a woman's partner will feel the anterior rim of a too-small diaphragm. A diaphragm that is too large will place pressure on the urethra, preventing the bladder from emptying completely and increasing the risk of urinary tract infection. A too-large diaphragm may also rub a sore on the vaginal wall. Diaphragms are available in diameters of 50mm to 105mm (about 2-4 inches). They are available in two different materials: *latex* (currently manufactured by Ortho and Reflexions) and *silicone* (currently manufactured by Milex and Semina). Diaphragms are also available with different types of springs in the rim.

Advantages

The diaphragm only has to be used during intercourse. Many women, especially those who have sex less frequently, prefer barrier contraception such as the diaphragm over methods that require some action every day.

Like all cervical barriers, diaphragms may be inserted several hours before use, allowing uninterrupted foreplay and intercourse. Most couples find that neither partner can feel the diaphragm during intercourse.

The contraceptive diaphragm may be used as a menstrual device, much like the commercial product, Instead. Contact with blood will discolour the diaphragm, but will not affect its contraceptive effectiveness. The diaphragm is less expensive than many other methods of contraception.

Disadvantages

Women (or their partners) who are allergic to latex should not use a latex diaphragm. Diaphragms are associated with an increased risk of urinary tract infection (UTI). Urinating before inserting the diaphragm, and also after intercourse, may reduce this risk.

Toxic shock syndrome (TSS) occurs at a rate of 2.4 cases per 100,000 women using diaphragms, almost exclusively when the device is left in place longer than 24 hours.

The increase in risk of UTIs may be due to the diaphragm applying pressure to the urethra, especially if the diaphragm is too large, and causing irritation and preventing the bladder from emptying fully. However, the spermicide non-oxynol-9 is itself associated with increased risk of UTI, yeast infection, and bacterial vaginosis. For this reason, some advocate use of lactic acid or lemon juice based spermicides, which might have fewer side effects.

HORMONAL CONTRACEPTION

Hormonal contraception refers to birth control methods that act on the hormonal system. Currently, all hormonal contraceptives are designed for use by women rather than men, though research on a male hormonal contraceptive ("the male Pill") has been underway for some time.

Hormonal contraceptives may be introduced into the woman's body in many different ways, among them orally, vaginally, transdermally, or through injections or implants.

Hormonal contraception may act in one or more ways to prevent pregnancy. It may cause ovulation to cease, preventing the possibility of fertilization; it may thicken the woman's cervical mucus, making penetration of the uterus by sperm more difficult; or it may alter and thin the endometrium so that a fertilized egg has difficulty implanting.

TYPES OF HORMONAL CONTRACEPTION

Oral Contraceptives

Combined oral contraceptive pill: known colloquially as "The Pill", is a combined estrogen and progesterone pill which is taken daily at the same time.

Progesterone-Only Pill (POP)

Most combined and progesterone-only pills may also be taken in high doses as emergency contraception (also known as the *morning after pill*). However, unlike plain copper IUDs, hormonal IUS is not approved for emergency contraception.

Non-surgical Devices

Contraceptive patch: It is an adhesive patch containing hormones which is applied to the skin and worn continuously. It is changed each week for three weeks and removed for one week.

Contraceptive vaginal ring ("NuvaRing"): It is a flexible ring containing estrogen and progesterone. It is inserted into the vagina and worn for three continuous weeks, removed for one week, then replaced with a new ring.

Intrauterine Devices

Progesterone IntraUterine System: otherwise known as the IUS, this device is inserted into the uterus by a healthcare professional, where it continuously releases progesterone. It remains in the uterus for a period of years, as determined by the manufacturer.

Surgical Devices

Implants: one or more flexible rods containing progesterone, are implanted under the skin.

Ormeloxifene

Ormeloxifene (also known as *Centchroman*) is sometimes mistaken for a hormonal contraceptive, probably because it is a pill that prevents pregnancy. Although it may be correctly termed a 'weekly contraceptive pill', it is not a hormonal contraceptive. Ormeloxifene is a *selective estrogen receptor modulator*, or *SERM*. It causes ovulation to occur sooner than it normally would, while causing the lining of the uterus to build more slowly, which, together, prevent pregnancy. Ormeloxifene is legally available only in India.

Advantages and Disadvantages

Because hormonal contraception represents a large group of diverse products, the advantages and disadvantages differ between different formulations. Generally speaking, if used properly, hormonal contraceptives are highly effective; except for abstinence, intrauterine device, vasectomy, and tubal ligation, no other method of birth control has as great a degree of effectiveness. Hormonal contraceptives also allow spontaneous intercourse.

On the other hand, hormonal contraceptives offer no protection against sexually transmitted infections. Like many other forms of birth control, hormonal contraceptives rely on the woman to use them correctly. Some, such as implants, require relatively little attention; others, such as injections or transdermal patches, require a schedule ranging from a week to several months. Still others—the wide varieties of oral contraception require a daily schedule. For example, many patient informations leaflet for these pharmaceuticals suggest using a back up method of birth control if 2 or more doses are missed. Information on the side effects and serious health risks can be located on the specific formulation's patient information leaflet. Finally, artificial contraception is objectionable to some religious traditions. These objections are furthered by the suggested, yet unproven post-fertilisation mode of action of preventing the implantation of a blastocyst.

INTRAUTERINE DEVICE

An intrauterine device (intra meaning within, and uterine meaning of the uterus) is a birth control device placed in the uterus, also known as an IUD or a coil (this colloquialism is based on the coil-shaped design of early IUDs). Dr. Ernst Gräfenberg of Germany invented an early IUD and was the first person to market these devices. The IUD is the world's most widely used method of reversible birth control, currently used by nearly 160 million women (just over two-thirds of whom are in China where it is the most widely used birth control method, surpassing sterilization). The device has to be fitted inside or removed from the uterus by a doctor or qualified medical practitioner. It remains in place the entire time pregnancy is not desired.

TYPES OF IUDS

There are two broad categories of intrauterine contraceptive devices: *inert and copper-based devices,* and *hormonally-based devices* that work by releasing a progestogen.

There are two types of intrauterine contraceptive available: the *copper Paragard* and the *hormonal Mirena.* Both of these contraceptives are referred to as IUDs.

Most non-hormonal IUDs have a plastic T-shaped frame that is wound around with pure electrolytic copper wire and/or has copper collars (sleeves). The Paragard T 380a is 32 mm (1.26") in the horizontal direction (top of the T), and 36 mm (1.42") in the vertical direction (leg of the T). In some IUDs, such as the Nova T

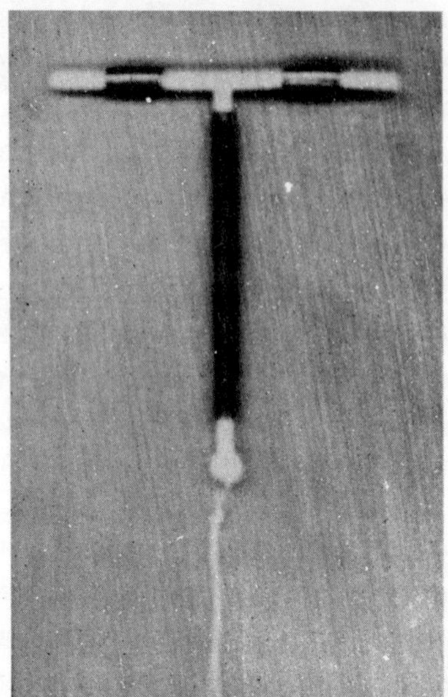

Fig. 4.2 *Intrauterine Contraceptive Devices*

380, the pure copper wire has a silver core which has been shown to prevent breaking of the wire. The arms of the frame hold the IUD in place near the top of the uterus. The GyneFix does not have a T-shape, but rather is a loop that holds several copper tubes. The GyneFix is held in place by a suture to the fundus of the uterus. All copper-containing IUDs have a number as part of their name. This is the surface area of copper (in square millimetres) the IUD provides.

Hormonal Intra-uterine Devices

Hormonal uterine devices do not increase bleeding as inert and copper-containing IUDs do. Rather, they reduce menstrual bleeding or prevent menstruation altogether, and can be used as a treatment for menorrhagia (heavy periods).

Although use of IntraUterine Systems results in much lower systemic progestogen levels than other very-low-dose progestogen-only hormonal contraceptives, they might possibly have some of the same side effects.

A lower-dose T-shaped IntraUterine System named Femilis is being developed by Contrel, a Belgian company. Contrel also manufactures the FibroPlant-LNG, a frameless IUS. FibroPlant is anchored to the fundus of the uterus as the GyneFix IUD is. Although a number of trials have shown positive results, FibroPlant is not yet commercially available.

Oral contraceptives are medications taken by mouth for the purpose of birth control.

Female

Two types of female oral contraceptive pill are widely available:

- The *combined oral contraceptive* pill contains *oestrogen* and a *progestogen*, and is taken once per day.
- The *progestogen* only pill contains only progestogen, and is also taken once per day. Side effects are— With no break in the dosage, flow does not initially occur at a predictable time. Most women tend to establish, over a few months, light spotting at approximately regular intervals. May cause mastalgia (breast tenderness) or mood swings. Weight gain is less commonly experienced than on COCP.
- *Other types of female oral contraceptive* are experimental or only available in limited areas:
  - *Mifepristone* is an antiprogestogen which has been used as a daily oral contraceptive in investigational clinical trials.
  - *Ormeloxifene* (also known as Centchroman) is a selective oestrogen receptor modulator which is taken one to two times per week. Ormeloxifene is approved as an oral contraceptive only in India.

Male

Male oral contraceptives are currently not available commercially, although several possibilities are in various stages of research and development.

BEHAVIOURAL METHOD

ABSTINENCE

Abstinence is a voluntary restraint from indulging a desire or appetite for certain bodily activities that are widely experienced as giving pleasure. Most frequently, the term refers to abstention from sexual intercourse, alcohol or food. In medicine, abstinence is the discontinuation of a drug, often an addictive one. This might, in addition to craving after the drug, be expressed as withdrawal syndrome. Abstinence from smoking is also recommended for those who undertake cosmetic surgery or have recently taken it.

COITUS INTERRUPTUS

Coitus interruptus, also known as withdrawal or the pull-out method, is a method of contraception in which a couple has sexual intercourse, but semen is ejaculated outside of and away from the vagina. Coitus interruptus may also more generally refer to any extraction of the penis prior to ejaculation during intercourse.

Disadvantages

Compared to the common reversible methods of IUDs, hormonal contraceptives, and male condoms, coitus interruptus is less effective at preventing pregnancy. As a result, it is also less cost-effective than many more effective methods: although the method itself has little direct cost, users have a greater chance cf incurring the risks and expenses of pregnancy and child-birth. Only models that assume all couples practice perfect use of the method find cost savings associated with the choice of withdrawal as a birth control method. The method is largely ineffective in the prevention of STDs, like HIV, since pre-ejaculate may carry viral particles or bacteria which may infect the partner if this fluid comes in contact with mucous membranes.

RHYTHM METHOD

Calendar-based methods are various methods of estimating a woman's likelihood of fertility, based on a record of the length of previous menstrual cycles. Various systems are known as the Knaus-Ogino Method, Rhythm Method, and Standard Days Method. These systems may be used to achieve pregnancy, by timing unprotected intercourse for days identified as fertile, or to avoid pregnancy, by restricting unprotected intercourse to days identified as infertile.

Advantage

The method is satisfactory for many women and men who find other methods unacceptable; offering it through family planning centres results in a significant increase in contraceptive use among couples who do not want pregnancy. The low cost of the method may also enable it to have a significant positive impact in countries that lack funding to provide other methods of birth control.

NATURAL FAMILY PLANNING

Natural family planning (NFP) is a term referring to the family planning methods.Periodic abstinence and the natural infertility caused by breastfeeding are the only methods deemed moral for avoiding pregnancy. When used to avoid pregnancy, NFP limits sexual intercourse to naturally infertile periods: during infertile portions of the menstrual cycle, during pregnancy, or after the menopause. Several methods may be used to identify whether a woman is likely to be fertile, which NFP users make use of to either try to avoid or to achieve pregnancy.

Methods

There are three main types of NFP: the symptoms-based methods, the calendar-based methods, and the lactational amenorrhea method. Symptoms-based methods rely on biological signs of fertility, while calendar-based methods estimate the likelihood of fertility based on the length of past menstrual cycles.

Symptoms-Based Methods

Some methods of NFP track biological signs of fertility. When used outside of the Catholic concept of NFP, these methods are often referred to simply as fertility awareness methods rather than NFP. The three primary signs of a woman's fertility are her basal body temperature, her cervical mucus, and her cervical position. Computerized fertility monitors may track basal body temperatures, hormonal levels in urine, or changes in electrical resistance of a woman's saliva.

From these symptoms, a woman can learn to assess her fertility without use of a computerized device. Some systems use only cervical mucus to determine fertility. Two well-known mucus-only methods are the Billings ovulation method and the Creighton Model Fertility Care System. If two or more signs are tracked, the method is referred to as a symptothermal method. Two popular symptothermal systems are that taught by the Couple to Couple League and the Fertility Awareness Method (FAM) taught by Toni Weschler.

Calendar-Based Methods

Calendar-based methods determine fertility based on a record of the length of previous menstrual cycles. They include the Rhythm Method and the Standard Days Method.

Calendar-based methods, which are sometimes considered NFP, but also not classified as NFP by the United States Conference of Catholic Bishops, have perfect-use failure rates of 5–9% per year, while symptoms-based and lactational methods of NFP have lower perfect-use failure rates: between 1%–3% per year. The common usage failure rate is up to 25% per year.

Lactational Amenorrhea Methods

The lactational amenorrhea method (LAM) is a method of avoiding pregnancy based on the natural postpartum infertility that occurs when a woman is amenorrheic and fully breastfeeding. The rules of the method help a woman identify and possibly lengthen her infertile period. A strict version of LAM is known as ecological breastfeeding.

STERILIZATION

Sterilization (also spelled sterilisation) is a surgical technique leaving a male or female unable to reproduce. It is a method of birth control.

Common Sterilization Methods

Vasectomy in males. The vasa deferentia, the tubes which connect the testicles to the prostate, are cut and closed. This prevents sperm produced in the testicles to enter the ejaculated semen (which is mostly produced in the seminal vesicles and prostate). Although the term vasectomy is established in the general community, the correct medical terminology is deferentectomy, since the structure known as the vas deferens has been renamed the ductus deferens.

Tubal ligation in females, known popularly as "having one's tubes tied". The Fallopian tubes, which allow the sperm to fertilize the ovum and would carry the fertilized ovum to the uterus, are closed. This generally involves a general anesthetic and a laparotomy or laparoscopic approach to cut, clip or cauterize the Fallopian tubes. Less commonly used is the Essure office procedure of inducing scarring and occlusion of the tubes by the effects of micro-inserts placed by a catheter passed through the cervix and uterus.

OTHER PROCEDURES THAT RESULT IN STERILITY

Hysterectomy in females. The uterus is surgically removed, permanently preventing pregnancy and some diseases, such as uterine cancer.

Castration in males. The testicles are surgically removed. This is frequently used for the sterilization of animals, with added effects such as docility, greatly reduced sexual behaviour, and faster weight gain (which is desirable in some cases, for example to accelerate meat production).

FEMALES STERILISATION

LAPAROSCOPIC SURGERY

Laparoscopic surgery, also called *minimally invasive surgery* (MIS), bandaid surgery, keyhole surgery, or pinhole surgery is a modern surgical technique in which operations in the abdomen are performed through small incisions (usually 0.5-1.5 cm.) as compared to larger incisions needed in traditional surgical procedures. Laparoscopic surgery includes operations within the abdominal or pelvic cavities, whereas keyhole surgery performed on the thoracic or chest cavity is called thoracoscopic surgery. Laparoscopic and thoracoscopic surgery belong to the broader field of endoscopy.

The key element in laparoscopic surgery is the use of a laparoscope. There are *two types*: a *telescopic rod lens system*, that is usually connected to a video camera (single chip or three chip)or a *digital laparoscope* where the charge-coupled device is placed at the end of the laparoscope, eliminateing the rod lens system. Also attached is a fiber optic cable system connected to a 'cold' light source (halogen or xenon), to illuminate the operative field, inserted through a 5 mm or 10 mm cannula or trocar to view the operative field. The abdomen is usually insufflated with carbon dioxide gas to create a working and viewing space. The abdomen is essentially blown up like a balloon (insufflated), elevating the abdominal wall above the internal organs like a dome. The gas used is CO_2, which is common to the human body and can be absorbed by tissue and removed by the respiratory system. It is also non-flammable, which is important because electrosurgical devices are commonly used in laparoscopic procedures.

Advantages

There are a number of advantages to the patient with laparoscopic surgery versus an open procedure. These include:

- reduced blood loss, which reduces the risk of needing a blood transfusion.
- smaller incision, which reduces pain and shortens recovery time.
- less pain, leading to less pain medication needed.
- Although procedure times are usually slightly longer, hospital stay is less, and often with a same day discharge which leads to a faster return to everyday living.
- reduced exposure of internal organs to possible external contaminants thereby reduced risk of acquiring infections.
- can be used in *gamete intrafallopian transfer* (GIFT) surgery to put the eggs back into the Fallopian tubes.

MINIMALLY INVASIVE PROCEDURE

A minimally invasive procedure is any procedure (surgical or otherwise) that is less invasive than open surgery used for the same purpose. A minimally invasive procedure typically involves use of laparoscopic devices and remote-control manipulation of instruments with indirect observation of the surgical field through an endoscope or similar device, and are carried out through the skin or through a body cavity or anatomical opening. This may result in shorter hospital stays, or allow outpatient treatment. However, the safety and effectiveness of each procedure must be demonstrated with randomized controlled trials. A minimally invasive procedure is distinct from a non-invasive procedure such as external imaging instead of exploratory surgery.

FAMILY WELFARE PROGRAMME

India launched the National Family Welfare Programme in 1951 with the objective of "reducing the birth rate to the extent necessary to stabilise the population at a level consistent with the requirement of the National economy".

The Family Welfare Programme in India is recognised as a priority area, and is being implemented as a 100% Centrally-sponsored programme. As per Constitution of India, Family Planning is in the Concurrent list. The approach under the programme during the First and Second Five-Year Plans was mainly "clinical" under which facilities for provision of services were created. However, on the basis of data brought out by the 1961 census, clinical approach adopted in the first two plans was replaced by "Extension and Education Approach" which envisaged expansion of services facilities along with spread of message of small family norm.

The estimates of population requiring various family welfare services as on 2001 are given below:

Total eligible couples (wife in the reproductive age group of 15-44)	177 millions
Total no. of pregnant women	29.5 millions
Total no. of new borns	26.8 millions
Total no. of children 0-6 Years as per Census 2001	158 millions

EVOLUTION OF FAMILY WELFARE PROGRAMME

The Family Welfare Programme during VII five-year plan (1985-90) was continued on a purely voluntary basis with emphasis on promoting spacing methods, securing maximum community participation and promoting maternal and child healthcare. In order to provide facilities/services nearer to the door steps of population, the following steps/initiatives were taken during the VII Plan period.

- The population in plain areas and for 3000 population in hilly and tribal areas. At the end of VII Plan, i.e., 31.3.1990, 1.30 lakhs sub-centres were established in the country.
- The Post Partum programme was progressively extended to sub-district level hospitals. At the end of VII Plan, 1012 sub-district level hospitals and 870 Health Posts were established in the country.
- The Universal Immunization Programme started in 30 Districts in 1985-86 was extended to cover all the districts in the country by the end of the VII Plan.
- A project for improving Primary Health Care in urban slums in the cities of Bombay and Madras was taken up with assistance from World Bank.
- Area Development Projects were implemented in selected districts of 15 major States with assistance from various Donor Agencies.

The achievements of the Family Welfare Programme at the end of the VII Plan were:

- Reduction in crude birth rate from 41.7 (1951-61) to 30.2.
- Reduction in total fertility rate from 5.97 (1950-55) to 3.8.
- Reduction in infant mortality rate from 146 (1970-71) to 80.
- Increase in Couple Protection Rate from 10.4% (1970-71) to 43.3%.
- Setting up of a large network of service delivery infrastructure, which was virtually non-existent at the inception of the programme.

- Over 118 million births were averted by the end of March, 1990.

The approach adopted during the Seventh Plan was continued during 1990-92. For effective community participation, Mahila Swasthya Sanghs at village-level was constituted in 1990-91. MSS consists of 15 persons, 10 representing the varied social segments in the community and five functionaries involved in women's welfare activities at village-level such as the Adult Education Instructor, Anganwari Worker, Primary School Teacher, Mahila Mukhya Sevika and the Dai. Auxiliary Nurse Midwife(ANM) is the Member-Convenor. A major new initiative undertaken during 1991-92 was the Child Survival and Safe Motherhood Project, an integration of Universal Immunization Programme with expanded/intensified MCH activities in high IMR States/Districts of the country.

To impart new dynamism to the Family Welfare Programme, several new initiatives were introduced and ongoing schemes were revamped in the VIII Plan (1992-97). The broad features of these initiatives are as under:

World Bank assisted Area Projects which seek to upgrade infrastructure and development of trained manpower have been continued during the VIII Five Year Plan. Two new Area Projects namely India Population Project (IPP)-VIII and IX have been initiated during the VIII Plan. The IPP-VIII project aims at improving health & family welfare services in the urban slums in the cities of Delhi, Calcutta, Hyderabad and Bangalore. IPP-IX will operate in the States of Rajasthan, Assam and Karnataka.

An USAID assisted project named "Innovations in Family Planning Services" has been taken up in Uttar Pradesh with specific objective of reducing TFR from 5.4 to 4 and increasing CPR from 35% to 50% over the 10 years project period.

Recognising the fact that demographic and health profile of the country is not uniform, 90 districts which have CBR of over 39 per thousand (1991 census) were identified for differential programming. Enhanced allocation of financial resources, amounting to Rs. 50 lakhs per year per district, was made for upgradation of health infrastructure in these districts from 1992-93 to 1995-96. This amount is being used for providing well-equipped Operation Theatres, Labour Room, a six-bedded observation ward and residential quarters for paramedical workers in 5 PHCs of each district per year. All the block level PHCs of these 90 districts have been covered.

Realising that Government efforts alone in propagating and motivating the people for adaptation of small family norm would not be sufficient, greater stress has been laid on the involvement of NGOs to supplement and complement the Government efforts. Four new schemes for increasing the involvement of NGOs have been evolved by the Department of Family Welfare.

The Universal Immunisation Programme (UIP) was launched in 1985 to provide universal coverage of infants and pregnant women with immunisation against identified vaccine preventable diseases. From the year 1992-93, the UIP has been strengthened and expanded into the Child Survival and Safe Motherhood (CSSM) Project. It involves sustaining the high immunisation coverage level under UIP, and augmenting activities under Oral Rehydration Therapy, prophylaxis for control of blindness in children and control of acute respiratory infections. Under the Safe Motherhood component, training of traditional birth attendants, provision of aseptic delivery kits and strengthening of first referral units to deal with high risk and obstetric emergencies are being taken up.

The targets fixed for the VIII Plan of a National level birth rate of 26 was achieved by all States except the States of Assam, Bihar, Haryana, Madhya Pradesh, Orissa, Rajasthan and Uttar Pradesh.

IX FIVE-YEAR PLAN (1997-2002)

Reduction in the population growth rate has been recognised as one of the priority objectives during the IX Plan period. The objectives during the IX Plan are:

- To meet all the felt-needs for contraception
- To reduce the infant and maternal morbidity and mortality. So that there is a reduction in the desired level of fertility.

The strategies during the IX Plan will be:

- To assess the needs for reproductive and child health at PHC level and undertake area-specific micro planning.
- To provide need-based, demand-driven, high quality, integrated reproductive and child healthcare.

ROLE OF PHARMACIST IN FAMILY PLANNING

Health is a word very familiar to us but it also carries a lot of complications and problems. According to the World Health Organisation, health is a state of complete physical, mental and social well-being and not merely absence of any illness. To make the above definition of health practical we have to depend upon a "healthcare team".

A healthcare team is the group of people who share a common health goal and common objectives determined by community needs. India with the greatest cultural diversity, health though an important issue is being neglected due to many hindrances. The condition is further worsened due to insignificant drug use problems. On the spurge of many spurious, duplicate and adulterated drugs, it is in the hands of the pharmacist particularly the community pharmacist, to take up the challenge for providing better healthcare and better outcomes economically.

ROLE OF COMMUNITY PHARMACIST

A community pharmacist is the professional who would be in direct access to the public and whose duties are widely sought after by the public and patients. He dispenses medicines with a prescription and in certain cases without a prescription where applicable (OTC drugs). As he is the person who will be in direct contact with the public, he has to play an important role in decreasing the mortality and morbidity in the public.

Community pharmacy practice evolved in the post-second World War period. A pharmacist not only began to perform functions that were new to pharmacy, but they began to innovate functions and make original contribution to literature. The popular motto of "patient-oriented practice" and "drug-use control" came into practice. But unfortunately the role of community pharmacist is not so much recognized till today especially in India and needs strong efforts.

Although community pharmacist is of key importance in providing better healthcare, it is the matter of shame for us that the Indian patient does not find any difference between the grocer and the pharmacist. Despite of major role of community pharmacy, the situation and condition of the community pharmaceutical service has stood where it was like a man walking on a treadmill. He walks and walks and sweats, but remains in the same place. Until and unless the link between the people and physician, i.e., the pharmacist does not get its proper recognition any dreams of making India, a healthier nation cannot be fulfilled.

The need of the hour is to make community pharmacist a key towards better healthcare. The community pharmacist can take part in health promotion campaigns, locally and nationally, on a wide range of drug-related and health-related topics. A community pharmacist involvement could play an important role in the following areas of healthcare.

Nutrition Counselling

Community pharmacist can make, significant contributions in assuring adequate nutrition by advising his patients about basic food needs, keeping to correct improper food habits in children, advising on special requirements, suggesting special diet instructions for diabetic patients and people with food allergy and participating in school lunch programmes and schemes like mid-day meals etc. in rural areas.

There are certain facts such as women who often eat fish or omega-3-fatty acids are less likely to suffer stroke, symptoms of hyper vitaminosis result in irregular menstrual cycle and excessive intake during pregnancy may cause birth defects. The pharmacist can tell these facts to people to ensure better health. Nowadays designer foods, i.e., nutraceuticals/dietary supplements have not only gained considerable acceptance but also have new-found use and applications. They are considered to provide medical or health benefits. The community pharmacist could explain these new innovative products and their standardization.

Women Welfare-Pregnancy and Infant Care

A famous Sanskrit Shloka from Manusmriti scriptures goes as "Yatra Nariyastu Poojayanta, Ramante Tatra Deva" which means, "where women are worshipped Gods preside there".

Women are the cornerstone for effective public health and investing in women translate into investing in family, community and the Nation. Against the backdrop of a hectic and demanding schedule, women's health receives the least priority when it should be the first.

A woman goes through different stages throughout her life, each of which has specific need and the presence of a counsellor is needed in each one of them. The pharmacist who understands the normal course of pregnancy and infancy is at a distinct advantage as he or she can guide the mother in simple matters of hygiene and management. The community pharmacist can encourage breastfeeding and can play a major role by guiding the mother for the protection of the child by following proper immunization schedule. Efforts are definitely underway in this area.

Rational Use of Drugs

A community pharmacist can also advise on the administration of the medication, provide information on the storage of the medication and wherever necessary he can counsel the patient. Education regarding the disadvantage of polypharmacy can also be given to the patient. Drug information system should be set up and access to adverse drug reaction system should be made. A community pharmacist should do therapeutic drug monitoring and he should have a sound knowledge of genotype reporting, i.e., predictive pharmacology.

Drug information awareness programmes should be conducted to make people aware of side effects of certain OTC drugs, e.g., Aspirin — a wonder drug also has many side effects like gastric ulceration; asthma and large doses may cause tinnitus. Regular use of paracetamol can cause harm to the liver. How many amongst the common people know that drugs such as Action 500, Coldarin can increase blood pressure in patients having hypertension. Even pain shows difference between men and women. Where women respond better to the opiods such as morphine, pentazocine and pethidine men respond better to the non-steroidal anti-inflammatory drug, ibuprofen. Considering the above examples, in the best interest of public health a community pharmacist can provide counselling to common people unaware of these side effects.

Moreover, the definition of an OTC product should be that "which does not require the prescription of a registered medical practitioner but which can be sold only under the supervision of a pharmacist". In a nutshell there should be rational use of drug, i.e., right drug in right patient in right dose at right time. A community pharmacist is one of the inevitable members of the healthcare team who can help to achieve the goal of rational use of drugs by following good pharmacy practices. It is found that interventions by pharmacists in explaining the patients about medicines prescribed to them can significantly enhance patient knowledge of correct use of medicines from 56 per cent to 90 percent.

There is yet another role of the community pharmacist in India and that is enhancing the availability of essential drugs. Nearly 70% population in India is deprived of essential drugs for a variety of reasons including non-availability of health professionals and improper professional advice about the usage of drugs.

In India, one pharmacist for two thousand persons can improve access to medicines and their safe utilizations. The existing pool of community pharmacists can become an important instrument in bringing about this change. For setting higher standard for pharmacy practice in the country, the essential drug list should be received by the government and the availability of the essential drugs should be enhanced through the pharmacists.

Sexually Transmitted Diseases—AIDS

India has 3.5 million HIV positive cases, which is about 10% of the global HIV cases and barely second to South Africa. HIV drugs are expensive and beyond the reach of common man. Huge resource of community pharmacist can educate people in the prevention and information of HIV/AIDS. For this, Federation of Indian Pharmacists project in India on involvement of pharmacist in fight against AIDS is very relevant.

Another sensitive issue is the increasing number of women patients suffering from AIDS. The number rose from 7% in 1985 to 18% in 1995. Although many classes of antiretroviral are available like protease inhibitors, nucleoside reverse transcriptase inhibitors and non-nucleoside reverse transcriptase inhibitors, patients need close monitoring and strict dietary regimen. Explaining to what HIV is, its transmission, risk reduction, patient counselling are the components of the counselling that a community pharmacist can provide.

Alcohols, Drug Abuse and Smoking Cessation

The diseases of alcoholism and drug abuse also come under the purview of the community pharmacist. The pharmacist has a key-role to help individuals who become dependent upon alcohol. Drug abuse is similar to alcoholism yet different because it has been gaining more acceptances among young people. Annual mortality from tobacco-use exceeds that from all other causes combined. Smoking is the greatest single preventable cause of morbidity and mortality in India. It is the responsibility of a community pharmacist to take an active role in helping the smokers to stop smoking. Following a number of smoking policies through out the pharmacy, by written information and posters, can do this. The pharmacist can advise on the products available to assist the patient in giving up smoking. Counselling sessions can be made by the community pharmacist to stop smoking.

Family Planning

One of the greatest needs of the hour is to control the tremendously increasing population in India. A community pharmacist is the one who can control this rising population by counselling with people and doing programmes which exhibit the problems related with large families. He can tell the various families planning measures that are available in the market at affordable prices. He can educate the people and convince them about the advantages of having small families. So, like all other aspects community pharmacist plays a very important role in this case also.

Individualization of Drug Therapy

Today the latest concept in medicine is towards individualization of drug therapy. Where judicious patient care is needed individualization of drug therapy becomes a need, and a pharmacist can play a vital role in this. A physician who is preoccupied with patient diagnosis and treatment may not spare time for patient counselling regarding pharmaco-economics, drug information, alternative therapy, moral supporting etc. A pharmacist can set up a separate consultation room and provide counselling to the patient. He can store the details of patient history, allergies and other details necessary for therapy so that the concept of individualization of drug therapy could be implemented.

The ideal frontline pharmacist of the future has been described as a seven star pharmacist—someone who is equal in excellence to a five-star hotel yet accessible to everyone from the richest to the poor. The future 7-star pharmacists will have seven principal roles to play:

- Care giver;
- Decision-maker;
- Communicator;
- Leader;
- Manager;
- Lifelong learner; and
- Role model.

The community pharmacist with the above skills and attitudes should make himself an indispensable partner in healthcare system of a nation.

Conculsion

In the Indian healthcare system, pharmacist is underutilized because community pharmacy and pharmacy practice are yet to be established strongly and pharmacists working in community pharmacies do not provide patient counselling in the usual situation. We need to work closely with the pharmacist associations and share our common experiences and frame appropriate guidelines for India so that community pharmacist who plays a major role in providing better health care can be recognized.

In a nutshell, pharmacist in the healthcare system is like circumcentre of a triangle with physicians, patients and nurses at the corners of the triangle. He has direct contact with all healthcare professionals and patients. It is really important to appreciate the fact that a patient finds himself to be much more comfortable in a drug store than in a physician's dispensary. The role of community pharmacist is indispensable in providing better health care. Steps should be taken by the government and the pharmacist himself to make his recognition in the community as a better healthcare provider. The National pharmaceutical associations like Indian Pharmacists Organization, Federation of Indian Pharmacists, Indian Hospital Pharmacists Association and All India Organization of Chemists and Druggists etc. will have to be committed to change and use their influence to convince community and the government that pharmacists can play a significant role in national healthcare programmes.

STUDY QUESTIONS

1. What do you mean by Demography?
2. Explain the Contraceptive methods of Family Planning
3. Write short notes on the following:
   (a) Fertility;
   (b) Intrauterine device;
   (c) Natural Family Planning; and
   (d) Hormonal contraception.

■■■

5

FIRST AID

INTRODUCTION TO FIRST AID

First Aid is the most important branch of medical science. First aid is, like medicine, both an art and a science. The immediate and temporary treatment given to the person who suffers an accident or any sudden illness before the medical help (aid) available, is called *First Aid*. *First Aid* can also be defined as the immediate and temporary care given to an injured or sick person until the services of a qualified doctor are obtained. Proper and immediate care is absolutely necessary to save life and mitigate suffering. General Esmarch (1823-1908) was the famous German Surgeon who first conceived the idea of "First aid". In 1877 St. John Ambulance Association of England was formed. In 1920, Red Cross Society of India was established. This is an age when technology has produced complicated machinery and swift means of transport.

IMPORTANCE OF FIRST AID

To give efficient first aid, one should have good knowledge of human anatomy and physiology of the human body and common sense and experience. The main objectives of first aid are:

1. The immediate objective of First aid at a given situation is to save the life of the individual.
2. It is the first objective of First aid to reduce pain and prevent further injury or complication.
3. First aid should help to avoid further injury. It should correct situations which tend to increase the original injury.
4. The First aid should form a basis for subsequent treatment by the doctor or the hospital staff.
5. It can be done by supplying details of accident, injury and the First aid treatment given etc. The ultimate aim of First aid is to prevent disability and death.

To obtain understanding of the working of the human body and its response to injury and illness. This would be a good introduction to the study of medical science in a practical way.

FIRST AID KIT AND EMERGENCY EQUIPMENT

To make your job easy, Casualty should be well-equipped. At home, school, buses, factories and cars there should be a First aid kit or bag kept ready for emergencies. Infact the contents of a First aid kit will vary according to the duties to be performed and the special needs of the occasion. The following list provides a basis for selecting equipment for:

(a) First Aid Kit

(i) Dressing;
(ii) Triangular bandages;
(iii) Roller bandages;
(iv) Cotton wool;
(v) A set of large safety pins;
(vi) A pair of scissors;
(vii) Dissecting forceps;
(viii) Graduated medication glass;
(ix) Torch;
(x) A cake of soap;
(xi) A small notebook and pencil;
(xii) Glucose, sweets or lump of sugar; and
(xiii) Smelling salts.

(b) Equipment

(i) Stethoscope;
(ii) E.C.G. machine;
(iii) B.P. apparatus;
(iv) Cardiac monitor;
(v) E.N.T. instruments;
(vi) Suction machine;
(vii) Weighing machine;
(viii) Thermometer;
(ix) Nebulizer;
(x) Pulse oximeter;
(xi) Knee hammer;
(xii) Sturing set;
(xiii) Cut-open set;
(xiv) Catherisation set;
(xv) Thoracocentesis set; and
(xvi) Tracheostomy set.

All the instruments shall be properly sterilised and equipment shall be checked frequently. The staff nurse must know functioning of all the equipment as they may be asked to operate some when there is mass casualty.

UNCONSCIOUSNESS

Unconsciousness is a serious state, so the patient's condition may cause anxiety and worry to the First aider. However, prompt, efficient action which secures a good airway and removes any obstruction such as blood, vomit or dentures may prevent complications and save the life of the patient. The primary cause the patient becomes unconscious is the immediate result of any injury or disease affecting the central nervous system. In psychogenic hysteria etc., the patients are not truly unconscious but appear unconscious.

LEVEL OF UNCONSCIOUSNESS

It is important that the level of consciousness is noted and timed. If there is any change in the level of consciousness, this must be noted and the time recorded. The levels described merge one into the other and there may be slow or rapid movement from one level to another. All these are of significance in establishing a diagnosis or assessing progress of the patient.

Lucid. The patient is cooperative and conscious.

Confusion. He is disorganized but will obey commands.

Semi-coma. The patient will only react to painful stimuli but not voice commands; unconscious.

Coma. There is no response to stimuli; deeply unconscious.

Glasgow coma Scale. This scale is widely accepted in hospitals and is an easily understood description of the level of consciousness.

Respiration. The breathing may be quick, shallow, stertorous (snoring) or irregular.

Eyes. Examination of the eyes and the pupils and their reaction to light is always of great value in establishing the diagnosis.

Pupil size. The pupils may be small (contracted) or large (dilated). They may be equal or unequal.

Pupil reaction. The pupils normally become smaller when exposed to light.

The *pulse rate must be noted*. A rapid pulse occurs in shock, fainting, collapse and sometimes concussion of the brain.

Odour of breath. The odour of the breath should be carefully noted, as it may supply a clue in a care of poisoning. The smell of alcohol should be noted but does not always indicate a diagnosis of drunkenness. The patient may be unconscious.

REASONS OF IMPAIRED CONSCIOUSNESS

There are many reasons why a person's level of consciousness might be diminished.

1. Cerebrovascular accident (CVA)
2. Fits
3. Diabetes
4. Acute infections and toxaemic states.

ASSESSMENT

The first step must always be to assess airway, breathing and circulation, before moving on to assessing level of consciousness.

A history of the event together with any relevant medical history should be obtained.

DROWNING

Drowning is the result of complete immerse of the nose and mouth in water. Water enters the wind-pipe and lungs, clogging the lungs completely. The aim is to get the casualty on to dry land with minimum danger to yourself.

Treatment: Choose the safest way to rescue the casualty. If possible stay on land and reach with your hand a stick or a branch or throw a rope or float. Swim to the casualty and tow him only if you are a trained life-saver, or if the casualty is unconscious, it is safer to wade, if you can, than to swim.

The aim of First aid is to draw out water from lungs and to give artificial respiration, turn the victim face down with head to one side and arms stretched beyond his head. Infants or children could be held upside down for a short period, raise the middle part of the body with your hands round the belly. This is to cause water to draw out of the lungs and give artificial respiration until breathing comes back to normal. This may have to go on for as long as two hours.

ROAD TRAFFIC ACCIDENTS

Road traffic accidents are increasing in number and in severity. With the development of high-speed motorways, multiple collisions and involvements are becoming more common, particularly in times of reduced visibility, fog, or torrential rain. Cars rapidly lose control by skidding on smooth surfaces such as ice and by aquaplaning on water.

When confronted with a road traffic accident you must first carefully assess the situation to make sure that you and your car are visible and not at risk of being hit by another vehicle. Pull well away from the traffic stream if possible, as many 'Samaritans' have been killed or severely injured.

Assess the position of the cars in the accident, turn off ignition and ensure no smoking, particularly if there is a smell of fuel. Detach the batteries, if necessary. Check the airway of any people who are injured, unconscious or trapped. Blood, vomit, or dentures may need to be cleared, and the position of the patient's head should he adjusted carefully to improve air entry. Quickly examine the patient, assessing fractures, shock and wounds. If there is excessive bleeding, treat this by the application of a firm pad and bandage, with supplementary splintage, if necessary.

FIRE

Fire spreads very quickly, so warn any people at risk and alert the Fire Service immediately. Without putting yourself at risk, do your best to help everyone if Fire occurs in a building or house. Shut the doors behind you, look for the notices giving the location of the Fire Exits and assembly points. Familiarize yourself with guidelines at your workplace.

A Fire needs three components to start it and keep it going. They are ignition (an electric spark or naked flame), a source of fuel such as petrol, wood, or fabrics, and oxygen (air). Remove any one of these and you break this triangle of Fire. For example, switch off electricity, remove combustible materials and shut door on a Fire, smother flames with an impervious substance such as blanket or wood.

Treatment: The casualty must be prevented from panicking and rushing outside. Any movement or breeze will fan the flames. Quickly lay the casualty down with the burning side uppermost and put off the flames by dousing the victim with water, or other non-inflammable liquid. Wrap the casualty tightly in a coat, curtain, blanket, rug or other heavy fabric. Then lay him on the ground. This starves the flames of oxygen (air) and puts them out.

BURNS

Burns are injuries that are caused from corrosive substance, from dry heat (like fire, flame), friction or by lighting. *Scalds* are caused by moist heat due to boiling water, steam oil. The key factors in burn pathology are the area of the burn, the depth of the burn, and any special areas of the body, such as the respiratory tract, that are involved.

The burnt area will almost immediately begin to lose fluid which is very similar to plasma in its composition. If sufficient fluid is lost from the burn, hypovolaemic shock will develop. The area of the burn is, therefore, crucial as it determines the volume of fluid lost. Area may be estimated using *Wallace's Rule of Nine.*

The Ist, IInd and IIIrd degree burns classifications are to be avoided as they are imprecise terms that can mean different things to different people. It is more appropriate and precise to describe the depth of burns as either *full thickness, partial thickness* or *superficial*.

CAUSES OF BURNS

(i) Burn due to Electricity;

(ii) Burn due to Chemicals; and

(iii) Burn due to Severe Body Area.

MINOR BURNS AND SCALDS

In the case of minor burns, first clean the area gently with clean water, submerge the burnt area in cold water, cover with dry dressing, do not apply cotton wool direct to the burnt area, give warm drinks, for example, sweetened tea or coffee.

The effects of both *burns and scalds* are the same. The skin may be reddened or blister formed or destruction of the skin, or the deeper tissues.

There will be severe pain. There is immediate danger from shock which may be severe and made worse by the intense pain and by loss of plasma into the burnt area. Later, there is danger from septic infection.

The areas of *burns and scalds*, including the clothing involved are for all intents and purposes sterile for a short period and try your best to keep them so, until medical aid is available. Always use prepared dry sterile dressings and great care must be taken in handling and applying them.

The dangers of a burn increase with its surface area (even if it is only superficial) and if one-third or more of the skin area is involved, the patient may become dangerously ill. In small children and infants even small burns should be considered as serious injuries and medical aid sought without delay.

ASSESSMENT

Assessment of the burns victim starts with the airway. The nurse should note whether the burns involve the face and neck areas, and whether there is any evidence of the patient having inhaled flames or hot gas. Such evidence would include soot in the nasal passages or blistering around the mouth and lips.

Some burns cause remarkably little pain; ironically they are usually the more severe full thickness burns as the actual nerve endings have been destroyed, but other burns can be extremely painful.

The area of the burn should be estimated, using *Wallace's Rule of Nine*. This rule divides the body area up into multiples of 9%. For small areas, the area of the patient's hand can be taken as 1% of the body area. Areas of superficial erythema and redness should not be included in this calculation.

The last point to estimate is the depth of the burn. The appearance will give some clue: a full thickness burn is typically a dull grey colour with tough leathery eschar tissue; a partial thickness burn is usually red or pink in colour. Sensation is absent in the full thickness burn but present in a partial thickness burn. This may be tested for with the pin prick method.

A sketch of the burn is a useful means of recording its extent; areas of suspected full thickness burn can be shaded in and labelled as such.

The appropriate *First Aid for burns* is irrigation with copious amounts of cold water. This will retard the process of tissue destruction due to heat and also afford the patient considerable pain relief.

RESUSCITATION

Resuscitation is the combination of the techniques used for sustaining lives of those patients whose spontaneous breathing and heart is stopped. This is also termed as *Cardiac Pulmonary Resuscitation (CPR)*. This is an emergency procedure every doctor must be aware of. The basics of CPR are the same to maintain airway breathing and circulation of the patient who have a cardio-pulmonary arrest.

First thing is to check any foreign body in the airway and it must be immediately removed. If the patient's airway is obstructed, all other considerations are of secondary importance and immediate intervention to clear the airway is required. Common causes of obstruction are vomitus, blood, inhaled material such as food or dentures, and soft tissue trauma affecting the neck or respiratory tract. This trauma can be caused by the inhalation of flames or of hot or noxious gases leading to burns of the trachea, by insect stings in the upper respiratory tract, or by a blow to the neck. The unconscious patient will be far less able to protect his or her airway than the patient who is conscious.

ASSESSMENT

Airway obstruction is the first step in assessing the A & E patient. Obvious respiratory distress, cyanosis, stridor, the history of the incident and the patient's level of consciousness are all relevant facts in assessing airway patency. The sound of the patient's voice is also important. Is it hoarse? Laryngoscopy should not be performed as it may provoke spasm of the epiglottis or vocal cords. Shining a pen torch into the open mouth is the most appropriate way to examine the upper respiratory tract. Frequency and depth of respirations are important parameters for the nurse to record.

POISONING

Poisons are any harmful substances which when taken into the body in large quantities can damage the organ of digestion or, if absorbed into the blood may affect the vital organs, cause harmful action on the human body, injuring health and even causing death. The majority of medicines if taken in excessive doses act as poison.

Poison enters the body through the mouth due to eating or drinking poisonous substances. It may enter through lungs by inhaling household or industrial gases. It may enter the body by injection into the skin as a result of bites and stings.

CAUSES OF POISONING

(i) *Accidental poisoning*—Due to contaminated food, poisonous fungi berries, clinical substance, overdoses and sleeping pills etc.

(ii) *Suicidal poisoning*—When a person ingests any harmful substance intentionally with a purpose to commit suicide.

(iii) *Homicidal poisoning*—It may be administered intentionally for killing enemies.

SOURCE OF POISONING

(i) Swallowed Poisons

Sometimes acids, alkalies, disinfectants etc., are swallowed by mistake. They burn the lips, tongue, throat, food passage and stomach and cause great pain.

(ii) Inhaled Poisons

Fumes or gases from charcoal stoves, household gas, motor exhausts and smoke from explosions etc., cause choking which may result in unconsciousness in addition to difficulty in breathing.

(iii) Injected Poisons

Poisons get into the body through injection, bites of poisonous snakes and rabies dogs or stings by scorpions and insects. Danger to life is again by choking and coma.

(iv) Household Poisons

Many substances found in and about the home can be poisonous. These include liquid soap, some cosmetics, white spirit, rat poison etc. Children who are not aware of the consequences of eating these substances, fall an easy prey to these poisons.

SIGNS AND SYMPTOMS OF POISONING

Signs and symptoms of poisoning will depend on the poison consumed. General signs and symptoms are—Burning pain in alimentary canal, feeling of thirst, blood stained vomiting, extreme diarrhoea, diminished urine output, cyanosis, cold skin, pulse rate fast and feeble, difficulty in breathing, perspiration, convulsions and many casualties fall unconscious.

FIRST AID IN POISONING

1. Poisoning is a serious condition, which threatens life. Casualty must be taken to the hospital at once or doctor be sent for, with findings and if possible the name of the poison must be written on a chit and sent to the doctor.
2. Aid vomiting by tickling the back of throat by inserting two fingers in throat or make him drink lukewarm water mixed with two tablespoons of common salt to a glass of water.
3. Do not induce vomiting if the poison was corrosive in nature. Corrosives are those chemicals which destroy or burn the tissues.
4. If the casualty is unconscious (i) Do not induce vomiting. (ii) Make the casualty lie on his back on a flat hard bed without any pillow and turn the head to one side.

SPECIFIC POISONS

(i) Food Poisoning

This is due to the contamination of food by bacteria. It may also be due to incorrect cooking and storing. The patient feels nauseated and may already be vomiting. The patient may be suffering from abdominal pain and may have headache.

(ii) Drug Poisoning

This is caused by an accidental overdose of drug abuse. Drugs can be inhaled, swallowed or injected into the body. The symptoms depend on the drug and the quantity taken. The pupils of the eye may be abnormally dilated or contracted.

(iii) Barbiturates

This is usually suicidal, though it may be accidental in children. They may eat sleeping tablets carelessly left around by the parents. The patient goes in to a deep sleep and then into coma with respiratory depression, low blood pressure, a quick and feeble pulse and a cold clammy skin emetic, given soon after the tablets are taken, will be effective as the drug has sedative action on the stomach.

(iv) Aspirin

It is used in large doses as a suicidal attempt. Its repeated and prolonged usage for the treatment of pain may irritate the lining of the stomach and produce haemorrhage. If taken in large doses, it may produce vomiting and its effect on the central nervous system is to produce confusion, convulsions, sweating, overbreathing etc. Extensive gastric bleeding may also occur. The emetic is effective because of the slow rate of absorption. So, a doctor may wash out the stomach with good results.

(v) Carbon Monoxide

Common sources are domestic gas, exhaust fumes from petrol engines etc. It may be accidental or suicidal. Giddiness, headache and tightness of the chest, loss of use of lower limbs and unconsciousness are common symptoms.

(vi) Poisonous Plants

Certain plants grown in our garden as well as in the forest are dangerous if eaten or if one comes into contact with them.

(vii) Alcohol Poisoning

Alcohol depresses the central nervous system. It affects different people in different ways. Patient's breath may smell of alcohol. Patient may be vomiting. The patient may be partly conscious or fully unconscious.

(viii) Industrial Poisons

As a result of failure of a chemical plant, the workers may come in contact with dangerous chemicals or gases. Most common industrial poisons are gases.

BITES AND STINGS

1. Snake Bite

In countries where there are many venomous snakes, identification of the snake is important to enable appropriate treatment to be given. If the snake has been killed, it should be taken with the casualty to hospital. If in a zoo, it can be identified on the spot. Most people will not die because of the venom but from fear. All snake bites are not fatal. Only a very small quantity of the venom might have been injected.

Symptoms and Signs—These depend to some extent on the particular venom, but general malaise, nausea, vomiting, confusion and difficulty with breathing and vision may be experienced. A shock state may develop. Small puncture wounds, usually two, may be visible at the site of the bite. As time passes, severe drooling of saliva may occur.

First Aid Treatment

Reassurance. Lay the casualty down. Call an ambulance immediately, stating that the casualty is a victim of snake bite. The bite is on the arm or leg, apply a constrictive bandage on the heart side of the bite, tight enough to obstruct and stop the flow of the venom to all the parts of the body. Do not tie it too firmly.

2. Dog Bite

Dog bites are sometimes very serious. They may cause infection. If the animal is suffering from rabies, it will be transmitted to the casualty. The condition is known as *Hydrophobia*. Therefore, the dog must be chained and kept under observation for seven to ten days. If the dog is healthy after this period, there is no danger of rabies.

First Aid Treatment

All dog bites must be treated as potentially as bite by a rabies dog. To prevent rabies or other infections, wipe the saliva away from the wound. Wash the wound thoroughly, with plenty of soap and water.

3. Insect and Spider Bites

Mites, ticks and leeches are found in marshes and jungles. These animals do not bite but attach themselves firmly to the skin. Mites and ticks may carry Typhus and may transmit it to the person. Leeches are normally harmless, but they suck blood from the victim.

First Aid Treatment

Don't try to remove the insects normally, their mouth parts may remain in the skin, due to that skin may get inflamed and infected. Put the burning end of a cigarette to the body of the ticks and leeches, they will fall off. Apply weak ammonia or bicarbonate of soda or antihistamine content. This will relieve irritation.

4. Stings of Bees, Rasps, Fleas and Hornets

The stings of bees, rasps etc., can cause a lot of pain. The area may swell. Sometimes, the person may suffer from shock. Stings, including those of jellyfish and certain fish such as the weaver, may be very painful but are not usually a threat to life unless:

1. The individual is allergic to the venom.
2. Many stings are suffered.
3. The sting is in the mouth or throat causing swelling which may obstruct the airway, causing asphyxia.

First Aid Treatment

A sting should be removed with forceps or with the tip of a sterilised needle. Apply weak ammonia or bicarbonate of soda or antihistamine ointment to the area. This will relieve the pain.

5. Bee and Wasp Stings

Following a sting, the poison sac and, in the case of bee stings, the sting itself will be left in the skin. It is essential to avoid squeezing the sac.

First Aid Treatment

Attempt to remove the sting with tweezers, if this can be done without exerting pressure on the sac. Use a magnifying glass if available to get a close-up view. Apply a cold compress. If there is persistent pain or swelling, seek medical aid.

ANAPHYLACTIC SHOCK

Some individuals are so sensitive to foreign substances, such as the from an insect sting or a certain drug, that large amounts of the histamine are released in the body. This causes swelling around eyes as well as at the site of the sting, difficulty with breathing and development of a shock state. This situation may occur within minutes.

First Aid Treatment

1. Call for an ambulance immediately.
2. Maintain an open airway.
3. Lay the casualty down; treat for shock.
4. Cardiopulmonary resuscitation may be required; monitor pulse and respiration frequently.

FRACTURE

Fracture is the breaking or discontinuity of a bone. It could be either a crack or complete fracture but both are technically termed as a fracture. Fractures are usually thought of as being due to trauma. This is not always the case, however, as repeated stress on a bone can lead to its fracture by a process similar to mental fatigue. Such a fracture is logically known as a stress fracture and is commonly seen in the foot (metatarsal) or the lower limb (fibula). Alternatively, bone can be so weakened by disease that it fails with little or no force involved. This is known as a *pathological fracture* and is seen, for example, where a tumour has led to secondary deposits in the bone (bony metastases).

The vast majority of fractures are due to trauma, and these are described as direct or indirect.

In an *indirect fracture,* the break occurs at some point other than that where the force impacted against the bone. For example, a fall on an outstretched hand may lead to a fracture of the clavicle or wrist.

Conversely, a *direct fracture* occurs when the bone breaks at the point of impact; thus, an over-the-ball-tackle in football leads to a fractured lower third of tibia and fibula.

Various Types of Fracture

If the fracture site is in direct contact with the outside environment, no matter how small the wound, it is an *open or compound fracture.* The importance of this consideration stems from the risk of infection which can involve the bone, leading to the very serious condition of osteomyelitis.

Closed or simple fracture in which a bone has been broken, but there is no serious injury to other important tissues in the vicinity. They are further classified as:

(a) *Transverse fracture*—In these the bone is broken almost straight across due to direct violence.

(b) *Spiral fracture*—In this the bone is obliquely broken due to indirect violence.

(c) *Fissured fracture*—In this the bone is cracked but not completely broken.

Complicated fracture is one when there is associated injury to some important internal structure, e.g., brain, spinal cord, lung, spleen etc., and when a fracture at a joint is associated with dislocation.

A *comminuted fracture* is one in which a bone is broken and there are more than two fragments, e.g., fracture of patella due to direct violence.

An *impacted fracture* is one when the fragments of a fracture are driven into one another and wedged firmly together. This kind of fracture occurs usually at the ends of long bones, e.g., upper end of humerus.

The *green stick fracture* occurs in children under the age of twelve. In this bone may be cracked and bent without breaking completely across.

A *depressed fracture* is one in which the broken part of the bone is driven inwards, e.g., when the vault of the skull has been fractured and a piece of the bone is pressed inwards. This may cause the signs and symptoms of compression.

SOME COMMON FRACTURES

FRACTURES OF THE UPPER LIMB

(a) Arm Bone (Humerus)

Humerus can be broken near the shoulder joint, middle part or near the elbow.

Fracture Upper End of Humerus

The fracture is slightly difficult to manage, as upper arm has got strong muscles and these muscles produce pull and overlapping of ends that get broken.

If the fracture is close to shoulder, place a pad in the axilia. Lightly tie the arm to the chest. Bend the elbow, and, with the hand on the opposite shoulder, apply a collar and cuffsling.

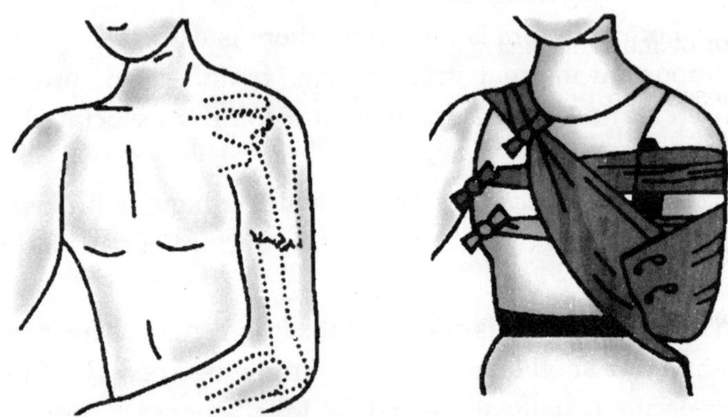

Fig. 5.1 *Fracture of upper arm.*

Fracture Middle of Humerus

There is likehood of shortening due to muscle pull. If the fracture is in the Mid Shaft, place a pad between arm and chest, one bandage above and the other below the site of fracture. Support the forearm in Collar bone, the sling.

(b) Fracture of Forearm

There are two bones, i.e., radius and ulna. Forearm fractures are the only fractures where external splintage is definitely required. *Coller's fracture,* near to the wrist, is very common. It is caused by a fall on the outstretched hand. There will be swelling and deformity at the wrist.

It is best to use a splint for First Aid in forearm fractures. A folded newspaper or magazine will serve well, if it extends from the elbow to the fingers.

Treatment—Place the forearm across the chest at right angle with thumb finger uppermost and palm of the hand towards the body. Roll the folded newaspaper or magazine around the forearm. Apply one bandage above the fracture and a second, as a figure of eight, around the wrist and hand. Support the arm in a sling with fingers, slightly higher than the elbow. Watch the fingers for signs of interference with the blood circulation, in which case, loosen the bandage slightly.

Fracture of the Hand and the Fingers

These fracture are mostly due to direct injury. There may also be severe bleeding into the palm if palmar arch (artial blood supply) is broken.

Tie the triangular bandage as for the crush injury of the hand. Use splint if available. Support the hand in broad arm sling.

Fractures of the Lower Limb

Femur

It is longest bone of the body. This bone could break at any place along its length or at the neck of the bone. Fractures of the neck is seen in old people with very mild cases like tripping or slipping in bathroom. Femur is common in elderly people. Fractures of the femur are always serious due to bleeding into the surrounding tissues.

The *signs and symptoms* of this fracture are pain, swelling and shock. Shortening of limb. The foot on the injured side, lies turned to the outside.

Treatment—Treat for shock. Pad between the legs and bring the good leg along side the injured one. Tie together the knees, ankles, hips, above and below the fracture. If there is a long and difficult journey to the hospital, two well padded splints should be applied. One, between the legs, the other, on the outside extending from axilia to the foot. Secure the splints with bandages around the chest, pelvis, knees, above and below the fracture, lower legs, a figure of eight around the ankles and knee.

Fracture of Knee Cap (Patella)

Fracture of the patella may occur due to direct force, but is more often, due to muscular action.

Signs and symptoms—The limb is helpless. There is much swelling. The gap may be felt between the two bits of bone.

Treatment—Support the casualty in a sitting position. Raise the injured leg gently and place the uninjured leg under for support. Tie the ankles together, and raise the legs on a box. The legs may be tied together by means of a narrow bandage above the knee in a figure of eight bandage. If a splint is available, apply it to the base of the limb, it should reach from the buttock to beyond the heel, pad under the ankle, and secure the splint to the limb by bandages round the thigh, ankle and figure of eight, above and below the knee.

Fracture of Lower Leg

The tibia only, or both and fibula may be broken. All the signs of fracture are seen in these cases. If the tibia only is much swelling around, the ankle fracture of ankle bones also, should be suspected.

Treatment—Treat as for femur fracture, but without the long splint. One or both of the bones may be broken. When both the bones are broken then pain, swelling, shock, etc., occurs, but when fibula only is broken no deformity is visible because it is splinted by the tibia. Fracture of bones of ankle should be suspected in swelling around the ankle.

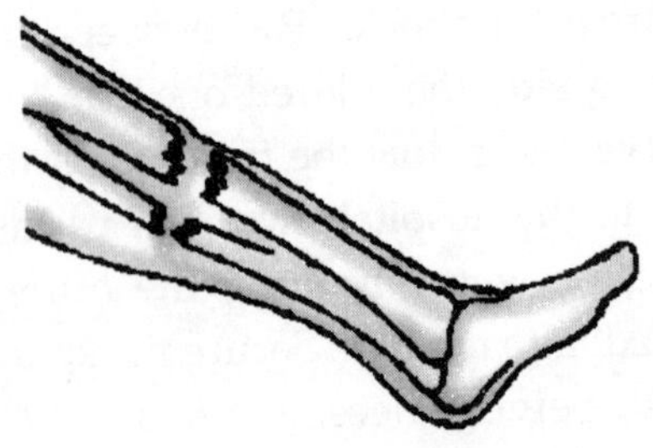

Fig. 5.2 *Fracture of lower leg.*

Fracture Foot and Toes

This fracture is caused by direct force, like a crush injuries due to heavy items falling on the foot or wheel passing over the foot. There could be wound and severe bleeding.

Treatment: Remove footwear and treat wounds. Raise and support the foot. Apply a padded splint to the sole of the foot. Secure the splint with a figure of eight bandage. Start with the centre of broad bandage on the splints, cross the ends over the instep and carry them to the back of the ankle and again cross once more, to bring them to the front of the ankle. Cross once more to bring the ends to the foot, cross and tie it off over the centre of the splint. Transport the casualty by stretcher with the foot raised.

Fracture of Skull Bones

Skull consists of 8 bones namely frontal, two parietal, occipital, two temporals, ethmoid and sphenoid. A direct blow or fall on the head, may cause fracture of the upper part of the skull, is often a depressed fracture. A fall on the feet or buttocks or a blow to the lower jaw may cause fracture of the base of the skull when blood or brain fluid may be seen coming from the ear or nose. Fracture of the skull may cause unconsciousness immediately or coming later.

Treatment—If breathing is not noisy, lay the casualty on his back with head and shoulder slightly raised. If breathing is noisy, place the casualty into the recovery position with head to one side. If there is bleeding from the ear, turn the head so that the bleeding side is down. Do not try to rouse the casualty. Keep him quiet and undisturbed. Keep the head still during transport, using sand bags or pads. Treat for shock and refer immediately.

Fracture of Rib

Ribs may be broken by direct force, or indirectly by a crush injury. There is danger that the broken ribs may be driven inwardly causing injury to the lungs.

Signs and Symptoms—Pain that is made worse by coughing or deep breathing. The casualty takes short, shallow breaths, so that, the ribs do not move and increase the pain. If the lung is injured, blood may be coughed up. If there is an open wound in the chest, air is sucked in and blows out as the casualty breathes. This is a serious complication.

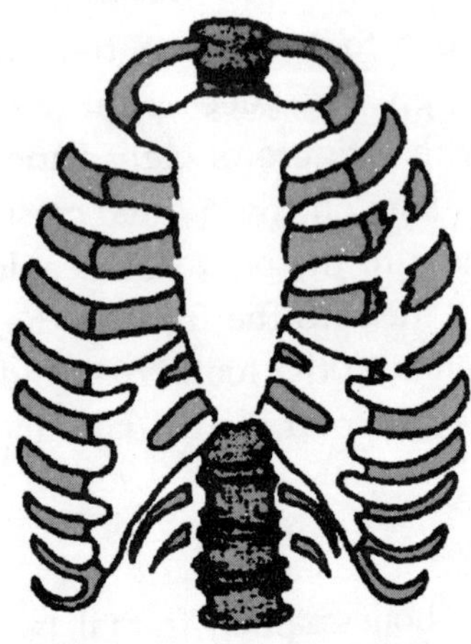

Fig. 5.3 *Fracture of ribs.*

Treatment—(a) If the fracture is *uncomplicated*—Apply two broad bandages to the area of pain. The upper bandage should overlap the lower one by half its width. Tie them lightly first after the casualty has breathed out, with knots near the front on the uninjured side. Support the arm to the injured side in a sling. (b) If the fracture is *complicated* —If there is a sucking wound, cover it with a dry dressing pad bandage firmly. In other cases, do not apply bandages. Support the casualty with head and shoulders raised and turned towards the injured side, transport carefully in the position on a stretcher. A sling may be applied to the arm on the injured side.

Fracture of Pelvis (Hip Bone)

Fracture of the pelvis, usually, occurs due to direct force such as in the crush injuries, road accidents (specially of two wheelers). Especially, the urinary bladder or urethra passage is the main organ of pelvic cavity, it may be injured causing urinary complication.

Signs and Symptoms—Pain in the hips when they are pressed together. The casualty is unable to stand, nor to move the legs without pain. There may be an urge to pass urine, but he is unable to do so or finds it difficult. There may be internal bleeding.

Treatment—Lay the casualty in the most comfortable position. If he wants to stand up on his knees, support them with folded clothing or pillow. Ask him to avoid passing urine. If a hospital is near, transport him on a stretcher without bandaging. If the journey is long and on rough roads, apply pads between the knees and ankles, then tie two overlapping broad bandages or a towel around the pelvis. Bandages should be tied on the uninjured side. Tie the knees together, with a broad bandage. Tie a figure of eight bandage around the ankles and feet.

Fracture of Spine

Spine or vertebral column is formed of a series of bones called vertebrae. In youth the vertebrae are 33 in numbers,

- 7 cervical (in neck)
- 12 thorax (in thorax)
- 5 lumber (in loins regions)
- 5 sacral (in the pelvis)
- 4 coccygeal (in the pelvis)

Sacral and coccygeal vertebrae are firmly united and are fixed while others are separate and movable. Spine has to bear the weight of the head and trunk.

Spinal fracture due to indirect force includes:

- Neck fracture in whiplash injuries, thrown forward suddenly in a moving vehicle. Pull on vertebrae while lifting heavy weights.
- Spinal fracture due to direct force includes:
- Fall of heavy weight on the back, falling from height on the back, earthquakes, landslides, stampedes in fairs etc.
- The casualty complains of pain at the side. The spinal cord may be damaged causing paralysis and loss of sensation below the side of the fracture. By good First Aid treatment, paralysis may be prevented.

Treatment—Warn the casualty not to move. Treat for shock. Get a long enough board on which the casualty can lie. Collect padding material, bandages and blanket or rug. Cover the board with a folded blanket and place small pillows or pads to fit the neck and middle of the back. Atleast four helpers are needed to get the casualty lying on the board. First place padding between legs. Tie together the ankies and feet with figure of eight bandage, and to his knees together.

When all are ready, the helper must carry together and be very careful not to bend or twist the spine as they either roll the casualty or lift him to get him on the prepared board. One should hold the head firmly and keep the neck straight. Another hold the legs near the ankles, while other keep the shoulder and hips steady and in line. Tie the casualty to the board to prevent movement during transport. If there is a neck injury, do not use a pillow under the neck, but place bags of sand or firm pads on each side of the bed to keep from moving. Take the casualty to hospital or health centre, as soon as possible.

BANDAGE

Bandage is used to protect or support the hurt part of the body. It is long piece of thin cloth which is wound around an injured part of the body. It should not be applied so tight as to cause injury to the part or to reduce the circulation of the blood. Bandages are used to maintain direct pressure over a dressing to control bleeding, to support for a limb or joint and restrict movement. It should be applied firm enough to keep dressing and splints in position. A bluish tinge and loss of sensation of the finger or nails may be the danger sign to indicate the bandages are too tight.

Types of Bandages

Standard bandages are made from gauze, muslin, flannel, rubber or adhesive, crinoline. For First Aid, bandages can be improvised by tie, stocking, scarf, handkerchief or saree falls. There are many types of bandages in use these days, First Aider requires to learn about *triangular* and *roller* bandages because they are easily available and do not require many precautions and skills.

(1) Triangular Bandage

(2) Roller Bandage

1. Triangular Bandage

It may be used in nursing and for slings to support an arm after injury. There are two types of triangular bandages—Reef Knot and Slings.

(i) Reef Knot

(ii) Slings

(a) Arm Sling

In arm sling triangular bandage is used as a whole cloth. It is used as a support to the limb after application of bandage, plaster of paris cast for the injured or fractured any part of upper limb.

(b) Cuff and Collar Slings

This bandage is applied at the wrist and tied at the neck. This sling is used to support the injuries or fractures of wrist.

(c) Triangular Slings

It is the modification of arm sling. It is used for supporting arm in cases of fractured collar bone.

Use of Triangular Bandages for Other Body Parts

(i) **Scalp**—Fold in a hem along the base of triangular bandage. Then place it on the forehead joint above the level of eyebrows. Take the two ends backwards after placing the body of the bandage over the head, the point hanging near the nape of the neck. Cross the two ends, take them forward round the ears to meet on forehead. Tie both these ends on the forehead making a reef knot. Pull the point firmly downwards and pin it to the bandage tucking the point inwards.

(ii) **Eye**—Place the centre of the bandage over the injured part (eye/ear) and wind the bandage around the part. Tie in a place away from wound.

(iii) **Hand**—Place the open bandage in such a way that the injury is uppermost. Place the fingers towards the point and the wrist above the base. Now turn the point over so that it reaches the wrist. Make a narrow inward hem, pass the ends around the wrist, cross over. Tie it up over the point. Turn the point over the knot and pin it.

(iv) **Wrist**—Place the centre of a narrow bandage across the palm of a hand. Collect the ends and carry them to the back of the hand leaving out the thumb. Cross the ends on the back of the hand and carry them around the wrist at the lower end of the forearm. Tie on the middle of the back of the limb.

(v) **Shoulder**—Place the centre of the open bandage on the shoulder with the point over the side of the neck. Take the ends around the middle of the arm and tie the knot on the outer side. Now take another triangular bandage and apply arm sling to the injured limb. Turn down the point of the bandage over the sling knot and pin it.

(v) **Elbow**—Bend the elbow to a right angle if it is safe to do so. Fold a suitable hem of the base of a triangular bandage and apply it as follows:

Lay the point on the back of the arm, in the middle of the base on the back of the forearm. Cross the ends in front of the elbow, then round the arm and tie the ends above the elbow. Turn the point down and pin it low down.

2. Roller Bandage

Roller bandages are used in hospitals and First Aid posts. Various sizes of roller bandages are available in standard first aid box. They are made of muslin, gauze, flannel, elastic and adhesive. The purpose of roller bandage is to secure dressing to cover the wounds, to provide support in case of sprains, to secure splints in cases of fractures or deformity.

BASIC BANDAGE PATTERNS

The roller bandage is applied by using singly or in combination with the five basic bandage patterns. They are recurrent, figure of eight, circular, simple and spiral.

1. **Recurrent Bandage**—The recurrent bandage pattern is used to retain a dressing on the head, on a stump or on the end of a finger. It is made by fixing the bandage with two circular

turns. The roll of bandage is then turned to cover the middle of the area. Next turns alternate on each side of the midline, passing back to front and front to back. Each turn overlaps one half the previous turn. When the entire area is covered, the bandage is ended with a circular turn directly over the first circular turn.

2. **Figure of Eight Bandage**—This bandage pattern is begun by forming two loops or turns, one above and one below a joint. Succeeding turns alternate above, where they descend, and below from where they ascend until the joint is covered. This pattern is modified to form the spica bandage, where one circumference is much bigger than the other.

Fig. 5.4 *Figure of eight bandage.*

3. **Circular Bandage**—In application of the circular bandage pattern, each succeeding turn overlaps the entire width of the previous turn. This pattern is used to secure the bandage at the start of tying a bandage.
4. **Simple Spiral Bandage**—The spiral bandage pattern is used to cover an area of uniform circumference. Each turn overlaps one-half or two-thirds of the previous turn. It is used for lower 1/3rd of forearm or leg.
5. **Spiral Reverse**—The spiral reverse bandage pattern is used on a cone shaped part such as the forearm or leg. After the bandage is secured by two circular turns, reverses (turning the bandage top to bottom) are made after each turn. Reverse pattern prevents gaps and ensures a smooth bandage.

CARDIAC ARRHYTHMIA

Cardiac arrhythmia is any of a group of conditions in which the electrical activity of the heart is irregular or is faster or slower than normal. Some arrhythmias are life-threatening medical emergencies that can cause cardiac arrest and sudden death. Others cause aggravating symptoms, such as an awareness of a different heart beat, or palpitation, which can be annoying. Some are quite minor and can be regarded as normal. In fact, most people have felt a skip of a beat or a sudden tachycardia, which are usually not a cause for alarm. Sinus arrhythmia is the mild acceleration followed by slowing of the normal rhythm that occurs with breathing. In adults the normal resting heart rate ranges from 60 beats per minute to 100 beats per minute. The normal heart beat is controlled by a small area in the upper chamber of the heart called the sinoatrial node or sinus node. The sinus node contains specialized cells that have spontaneous electrical activity that starts each normal heart beat.

ACUTE MYOCARDIAL INFARCTION

Acute myocardial infarction (AMI or MI), more commonly known as a heart attack, is a medical condition that occurs when the blood supply to a part of the heart is interrupted, most commonly due to rupture of a vulnerable plaque. It is a medical emergency, and the leading cause of death for both men and women all over the world. Important risk factors are a previous history of vascular disease such as atherosclerotic coronary heart disease and/or angina, a previous heart attack or stroke, any previous episodes of abnormal heart rhythms or syncope, older age—especially men over 40 and women over 50, smoking, excessive alcohol consumption, the abuse of certain drugs, high triglyceride levels, high LDL ("Low-density lipoprotein") and low HDL ("High density lipoprotein"), diabetes, high blood pressure, obesity, and chronically high levels of stress in certain persons.

The most common symptoms of MI in women include shortness of breath, weakness, and fatigue. Approximately one third of all myocardial infarctions are silent, without chest pain or other symptoms.

Immediate treatment for suspected acute myocardial infarction includes oxygen, aspirin, glyceryl trinitrate and pain relief, usually morphine sulfate. The patient will receive a number of diagnostic tests, such as an electrocardiogram (ECG, EKG), a chest X-ray and blood tests to detect elevated creatine kinase or troponin levels (these are chemical markers released by damaged tissues, especially the myocardium).

First Aid

As myocardial infarction is a common medical emergency, the signs are often part of First Aid courses. The emergency action principles also apply in the case of myocardial infarction.

SHOCK

ANAPHYLAXIS

Anaphylaxis occurs when a person or animal is exposed to a trigger substance, called an allergen, to which they have already become sensitized. Minute amounts of allergens may cause a life-threatening anaphylactic reaction. Anaphylaxis may occur after ingestion, skin contact, injection of an allergen or, in rare cases, inhalation.

Anaphylactic shock, the most severe type of anaphylaxis, occurs when an allergic response triggers a quick release from mast cells of large quantities of immunological mediators (histamines, prostaglandins, leukotrienes) leading to systemic vasodilation (associated with a sudden drop in blood pressure) and edema of bronchial mucosa (resulting in bronchoconstriction and difficulty in breathing). Anaphylactic shock can lead to death in a matter of minutes if left untreated.

Signs and Symptoms

Symptoms of anaphylaxis are related to the action of (IgE) and other anaphylatoxins, which act to release histamine and other mediator substances from mast cells (degranulation). In addition to other effects, histamine induces vasodilation of arterioles and constriction of bronchioles in the lungs, also known as bronchospasm (constriction of the airways).

Emergency Treatment

Anaphylaxis is a life-threatening medical emergency because of rapid constriction of the airway, often within minutes of onset, which can lead to respiratory failure and respiratory arrest. Brain and organ damage rapidly occurs if the patient cannot breathe. Due to the severe nature of the emergency, patients experiencing or about to experience anaphylaxis require the help of advanced medical personnel. First Aid measures for anaphylaxis include rescue breathing (part of CPR). Rescue breathing may be hindered by the constricted airways, but if the victim stops breathing on his or her own, it is the only way to get oxygen to him or her until professional help is available.

CARDIOGENIC SHOCK

Cardiogenic shock is based upon an inadequate circulation of blood due to primary failure of the ventricles of the heart to function effectively. Since this is a category of shock there is insufficient perfusion of tissue (i.e., the heart) to meet the required demand for oxygen and nutrients. This leads to cell death from oxygen starvation, hypoxia. Because of this it may lead to cardiac arrest (or circulatory arrest) which is an acute cessation of cardiac pump function.

Cardiogenic shock is *caused* by the failure of the heart to pump effectively. It can be due to damage to the heart muscle, most often from a large myocardial infarction. Other causes include arrhythmia, cardiomyopathy, cardiac valve problems, ventricular outflow obstruction (i.e., aortic valve stenosis, aortic dissection, systolic anterior motion (SAM) in hypertrophic cardiomyopathy), ventriculoseptal defects or medical error.

Signs and Symptoms

- Anxiety, restlessness, altered mental state due to decreased cerebral perfusion and subsequent hypoxia.
- Hypotension due to decrease in cardiac output.
- A rapid, weak, thready pulse due to decreased circulation combined with tachycardia.

- Cool, clammy, and mottled skin (cutis marmorata), due to vasoconstriction and subsequent hypoperfusion of the skin.
- Distended jugular veins due to increased jugular venous pressure.
- Oliguria (low urine output) due insufficient renal perfusion if condition persists.
- Rapid and deep respirations (hyperventilation) due to sympathetic nervous system stimulation and acidosis.
- Fatigue due to hyperventilation and hypoxia.
- Absent pulse in tachy arrhythmia.
- Pulmonary edema, involving fluid back-up in the lungs due to insufficient pumping of the heart.

Diagnosis

Electrocardiogram—An electrocardiogram helps in establishing the exact diagnosis and guides treatment, it may reveal:

- Cardiac arrhythmias
- Signs of cardiomyopathy

Radiology—Echocardiography may show arrhythmia, signs of PED, ventricular septal rupture (VSR), an obstructed outflow tract or cardiomyopathy.

Swan-ganz catheter— The Swan-ganz catheter or Pulmonary artery catheter may assist in the diagnosis by providing information on the hemodynamics.

Biopsy— In case of suspected cardiomyopathy a biopsy of heart muscle may be needed to make a definite diagnosis.

Treatment

In cardiogenic shock: depending on the type of myocardal infarction one can infuse fluids or in shock refractory to infusing fluids inotropica. In case of cardiac arrhythmia several anti-arrhythmic agents may be administered, i.e., adenosine, verapamil, amiodarone, ß-blocker. Positive inotropic agents, which enhance the heart's pumping capabilities, are used to improve the contractility and correct the hypotension. Should that not suffice an intra-aortic balloon pump (which reduces workload for the heart, and improves perfusion of the coronary arteries) can be considered or a left ventricular assist device (which augments the pump-function of the heart).

STUDY QUESTIONS

Write short notes on the following:

(a) Fracture of upper-end of Humerus;

(b) Fracture of Forearm;

(c) Fracture of the Hand and the Fingers; and

(d) Fracture of Ribs.

■■■

6

Environment and Health

INTRODUCTION TO ENVIRONMENTAL HEALTH

Good environmental health — in the areas of general habitat, water supplies, and sanitation facilities — is a basic requirement in all communities, including camps for displaced people. It is crucial for preventing many problems, yet is frequently ignored.

Shelter

Housing and general environmental conditions can have all important bearing on the outcome of emergency situations, especially as determinants of many diseases. In large-scale or countrywide emergencies it is impossible to make much change in these conditions in the short term but their importance should still be borne in mind with a view to appropriate improvements during the rehabilitation phase.

The creation of camps for refugees and other displaced populations should be avoided as far as possible, but where they exist already or have to be established (even if only temporarily), health aspects of the habitat they provide are a paramount consideration. Selection of appropriate sites should take account of the following factors:

(i) availability and accessibility of adequate water sources or existing drinking-water supply systems;

(ii) proximity of land suitable for agriculture (avoiding steep slopes and land prone to erosion);

(iii) soil characteristics (digging of latrines) and topography (drainage of waste-water); and

(iv) physical accessibility of the area (roads, bridges, etc.); accessibility of local markets; facilities for solid waste disposal.

With regard to the housing environment, a number of features that have important direct or indirect effects on the physical and mental health of occupants have been identified:

(i) structure, including protection offered against extremes of temperature, noise, dust, rain, insects, and rodents;

(ii) qualitative and quantitative adequacy of water supplies;

(iii) facilities for disposal and subsequent management of excreta and liquid and solid wastes;

(iv) safety of the site, in terms of drainage, protection from contamination, etc.;

(v) avoidance of overcrowding as a means of limiting the potential for accidents and the spread of disease; and

(vi) indoor pollution from the fuel used for cooking and heating;

(vii) facilities for food storage (to avoid spoilage, infestation with insects, etc.); existence of disease vectors and hosts; use of the home as a workplace, which may involve storage and use of hazardous materials or equipment.

WATER

Water is the giver and sustainer of life. Our bodies are made up of almost 70% of the stuff; it's in our muscles, brains and lungs. It takes oxygen to our cells and allows our body to rid itself of wastes. In short, we can't live without it. When we diet, the breakdown of body fat and muscle produces waste material. Drinking 6-8 glasses of water daily will help the kidneys flush out these toxins and quicken the weight loss process. Just like crash diets make the body think it's starving because of severe cutbacks in food, not drinking enough water causes the body to go into survival mode and it will strive to hang on to every drop. The result is water weight gain, and it shows up as swollen hands, feet and legs. Again, the solution is drinking plenty of water, 6-8 glasses a day; so if you don't want to store water, drink water.

HEALTH IMPACTS OF WATER POLLUTION

Adequate supply of fresh and clean drinking water is a basic need for all human beings on the earth, yet it has been observed that millions of people worldwide are deprived of this. Freshwater resources all over the world are threatened not only by over exploitation and poor management but also by ecological degradation. The *main source of freshwater pollution* can be attributed to discharge of untreated waste, dumping of industrial effluent, and run-off from agricultural fields. Industrial growth, urbanisation and the increasing use of synthetic organic substances have serious and adverse impacts on freshwater bodies.

It is a generally accepted fact that the developed countries suffer from problems of chemical discharge into the water sources mainly groundwater, while developing countries face problems of agricultural run-off in water sources. Polluted water, like chemicals in drinking water causes problem to health and leads to water-borne diseases which can be prevented by taking measures even at the household level.

WATER SUPPLY

It is equally important to ensure the safety of water and provide adequate quantities. The amount of water needed by each person varies with the setting, but the following are the approximate needs:

Location/circumstances	*Volume per person per day*
Clinics, field hospitals	40-60 litres
Feeding centres	30 litres
Personal needs	15-20 litres

Water should be collected from the cleanest available source. In the case of a well, installation of a simple pulley device and provision of buckets will make raising the water easier. Water sources should be protected by the following measures:

(i) A fence or wall should be erected to keep animals away.

(ii) Drainage ditches should be dug uphill from an open well to prevent storm-water flowing into it.

(iii) People should not be allowed to wash in the water source; children should not be allowed to play in or around a source.

Latrines should not be located (or defecation allowed) uphill from or within 30 metres of a water source.

In addition, families should be instructed to:

(i) collect and store water in clean containers;

(ii) empty and clean out containers regularly;

(iii) keep each storage container covered and not allow children or animals to drink directly from a container;

(iv) prevent people (particularly children) from putting their hands into the containers;

(v) take water from a container using a dipper kept specially for the purpose. Water can be made safe by chemical treatment, commonly chlorine and chlorine-releasing compounds. These are available in several forms:

(a) bleaching powder (25% by weight of available chlorine when fresh); this deteriorates quickly when stored in warm and damp places;

(b) calcium hypochlorite (typically 70% by weight of available chlorine); this is more stable than bleaching powder;

(c) sodium hypochlorite (normally sold as a solution of strength approximately 5%).

The chlorine dose should be carefully determined, and it may be necessary to seek the advice of sanitation experts. Moreover, the indiscriminate distribution of chlorine tablets usually does little good and may actually be harmful (the tablets are dangerous if swallowed).

Where chemicals are not available, water may be boiled for 1 minute to kill harmful organisms. If the local water source is known to be contaminated, it may be possible to arrange for large quantities of clean drinking-water to be brought from elsewhere in drums or tank-trucks.

When it seems likely that emergency conditions will persist for some time, more permanent facilities should be sought urgently, including artesian wells, bore-holes, and pumping and filtration equipment. In any case it is essential to disinfect water, either at the source in the case of centralized production or in the household by chlorination or boiling.

TRANSMISSION OF WATER BORNE DISEASES

Water borne diseases spread by contamination of drinking water systems with the urine and faeces of infected animal or people.

This is likely to occur where public and private drinking water systems get their water from surface waters (rain, creeks, rivers, lakes etc.), which can be contaminated by infected animals or people. Runoff from landfills, septic fields, sewer pipes, residential or industrial developments can also sometimes contaminate surface water.

This has been the cause of many dramatic outbreaks of faecal-oral diseases such as cholera and typhoid. However, there are many other ways in which faecal material can reach the mouth, for instance on the hands or on contaminated food. In general, contaminated food is the single most common way in which people become infected.

The germs in the faeces can cause the diseases by even slight contact and transfer. This contamination may occur due to floodwaters, water runoff from landfills, septic fields, and sewer pipes.

WATER-BORNE DISEASES

Water-borne diseases are infectious diseases spread primarily through contaminated water. Though these diseases are spread either directly or through flies or filth, water is the chief medium for spread of these diseases and hence they are termed as water-borne diseases.

BACTERIAL INFECTIONS

- *Botulism*—Clostridium botulinum bacteria – gastro-intestinal food/water-borne; can grow in food.

- *Campylobacteriosis.*
- *Cholera* — Vibrio cholerae bacteria — gastro-intestinal often water-borne.
- *Chronic granulomatous disease* — caused by the Mycobacterium marinum infection and localized in skin, frequently occurred with aquarium keepers.
- *Diarrheal* disease due to *E. coli.*
- *Dysentery* — Shigella/Salmonella bacteria — gastro-intestinal food/water.
- *Legionellosis* — cause Pontiac fever and Legionnaires' disease.
- *Leptospirosis.*
- *Otitis externa* — "Swimmer's Ear" .
- *Typhoid* — Salmonella typhi bacteria — gastro-intestinal water/food borne. Salmonellosis — due to many Salmonella species. Water/food/direct contact borne.
- *Vibrio* illness caused by the bacteria of vibrio vulnificus, vibrio alginolyticus and vibrio parahaemolyticus commonly found in seafood and recreational water.

Viral infections

Infectious Hepatitis (jaundice)

Poliomyelitis.

VIRAL INFECTIONS

- *Adenovirus infection* — its serotypes are typically water-borne.
- *Astroviruses.*
- *Caliciviruses.*
- *Circoviruses* — its human form of Transfusion Transmitted virus found in faeces, saliva, skin and hair.
- *Coronaviruses* — cause SARS and excreted in the faeces.
- *Enteric Adenoviruses.*
- *Hepatitis A* — Hepatitis A virus — gastro-intestinal water/food borne
- *Parvoviruses* — associated with Gastroenteritis.
- *Picobimaviruses* — associated with Gastroenteritis in AIDS patients, children and elderlies.

- *Polio* — polioviruses — gastro–intestinal exposure to untreated
- *Polyomaviruses* — its human form of JC virus cause Progressive multifocal leukoencephalopathy and detected in sewage.

ALLERGIC INFECTIONS

- *Hay fever* — a part of disease rate is associated with the high frequency of swimming pool attendance in childhood.
- *Meningitis.*
- *Trihalomethanes* — a byproduct of chlorinated water which will cause bladder cancer through inhalation and dermal absorption during showering, bathing, and swimming in pools.

PREVENTION OF WATER-BORNE DISEASES

Clean water is a pre-requisite for reducing the spread of water-borne diseases. It is well recognised that the prevalence of water-borne diseases can be greatly reduced by provision of clean drinking water and safe disposal of faeces.

Water is disinfected to kill any pathogens that may be present in the water supply and to prevent them from growing again in the distribution systems. Disinfection is then used to prevent the growth of pathogenic organisms and to protect public health and the choice of the disinfect depends upon the individual water quality and water supply system.

Without disinfection, the risk from water-borne disease is increased.

The two most common methods to kill micro-organisms in the water supply are -

(i) Oxidation with chemicals such as chlorine or ozone.

(ii) Irradiation with Ultra-violet (UV) radiation.

AIR

Air is a mixture of gases in the lower atmosphere. Dry air at sea level is composed in volume of nitrogen (78.08%), oxygen (20.95%), argon (0.93%), carbon dioxide (0.03%), together with very small amounts of other gases. Water vapour is found in variable concentrations.

AIR POLLUTION

Air pollution is a general term used to describe the mixture of substances that are naturally or artificially introduced into the air. The most well-documented of these substances (and those usually monitored on a routine basis) include sulphur dioxide (SO_2), nitrogen oxides (NOx, including NO and NO_2), carbon monoxide (CO), ozone (O_3), lead (Pb), and total suspended particles (TSP) also known as suspended particulate matter (SPM) or black smoke (BS).

Pollutants in the air can create smog and acid rain, cause respiratory or other serious health illnesses, damage the protective ozone layer in the upper atmosphere, and contribute to climate change. Air pollutants can be particularly harmful to people belonging to high-risk groups such as children and the elderly.

An active person inhales 10,000-20,000 litres of air each day – about 7-14 litres per minute, although a person taking strenuous physical exercise (e.g., jogging) may inhale up to 50 litres of air per minute. A 3 year-old child at rest inhales twice as much air per unit body weight than an adult; thus as their airways are narrower, and their lungs still developing, problems as a result of breathing in pollutants are likely to be more serious and longer lasting.

HEALTH EFFECTS OF AIR POLLUTION

One way of classifying the health effects of pollutants is to make a distinction between *two broad categories*: *acute* (i.e., short-term) and *chronic* (i.e., long-term) effects. For each of these categories, the effects can range in severity from death to minor illness or discomfort.

For example, dust and other polluting particles in air can have acute effects, such as immediate irritations to eyes and throat, or hospitalisation and even deaths from respiratory failure or heart attacks, caused by severe episodes of air pollution.

For some pollutants there may be a threshold level of exposure, below which no health effect is evident, e.g. SO_2. For others, there may be no threshold, and some effect may occur whatever the level of exposure is, e.g. benzene.

SOURCES OF AIR POLLUTION

The *major sources* of air pollution are the combustion of fossil fuels (for energy generation, industrial processes and transportation), and of solid fuels, such as coal and wood, for domestic purposes.

Air pollution is different from other forms of pollution in that, once the pollutants are in the air, exposure cannot be easily avoided. If high levels of outdoor air pollution are occurring in a city, it may be expected that a large proportion of the population will be exposed.

Levels of air pollution may vary markedly even at the local level, especially in the case of ground-level emissions (e.g., from road transport). Short-term variations in pollution levels will also occur due to variations in emission activity. The level of total human exposure will vary depending on the proportion of time one spends outdoors, the ability of the individual pollutants to enter the indoor environment and the levels of pollutants generated indoors from cookers, paints, furnishings and building materials. Most people spend a much larger proportion of their life indoors than outdoors. Therefore indoor air pollution is a significant public health problem, especially for children.

AIR-BORNE DISEASES

Most of the respiratory tract infections are acquired by *inhaling* the air containing the pathogen. Micro-organisms in *droplets* and infectious *dusts* and *spores* can be easily disseminated through air. Some of the respiratory diseases, which have an air-borne mode of transmission are—

FUNGAL DISEASES

It consists of many types. They are following:

(i) Cryptococcosis

(ii) Blastmycosis
(iii) Coccidioimucosis
(iv) Histoplasmosis
(v) Aspergillosis.

VIRAL DISEASES

Air-borne viral diseases consist of different types. They are following:

(i) Common cold
(ii) Influenza
(iii) Measles
(iv) Mumps.

BACTERIAL DISEASES

(i) Diptheria
(ii) Tuberculosis
(iii) Legionellosis.

AIR-BORNE PRECAUTIONS

Patients who have or may have an infectious disease that is spread by the air-borne route must be placed on Air-borne Precautions in addition to standard precautions.

Air-borne Precautions require a negative pressure room in addition to a private room. Negative pressure rooms are specially designed to prevent the flow of air from the room into the corridors and common areas where susceptible persons may be exposed. This is accomplished through fans and vents that direct the airflow outside of the building and/or through HEPA filters.

DISEASES REQUIRING AIR-BORNE PRECAUTIONS

- Tuberculosis, Pulmonary (or laryngeal)
- Varicella (chickenpox)
- Herpes Zoster (shingles)
- Rubeola (Measles).

SOLID WASTES

Each household generates garbage or waste day in and day out. Items that we no longer need or do not have any further use for fall in the category of waste, and we tend to throw them away. *Segregation* is an important method of handling municipal solid waste. Segregation at source can be understood clearly by schematic representation.One of the important methods of managing and treating wastes is *composting*.

As the cities are growing in size and in problems such as the generation of plastic waste, various municipal waste treatment and disposal methods are now being used to try and resolve these problems. One common sight in all cities is the rag picker who plays an important role in the segregation of this waste.

Garbage generated in households can be recycled and reused to prevent creation of waste at source and reducing amount of waste thrown into the *community dustbins*.

Four Rs (Refuse, Reuse, Recycle, Reduce) to be followed for waste management:

1. *Refuse*. Instead of buying new containers from the market, use the ones that are in the house. Refuse to buy new items though you may think they are prettier than the ones you already have.
2. *Reuse*. Do not throw away the soft drink cans or the bottles; cover them with home-made paper or paint on them and use them as pencil stands or small vases.
3. *Recycle*. Use shopping bags made of cloth or jute, which can be used over and over again [will this come under recycle or reduce?]. Segregate your waste to make sure that it is collected and taken for recycling.
4. *Reduce*. Reduce the generation of unnecessary waste, e.g., carry your own shopping bag when you go to the market and put all your purchases directly into it.

TYPES OF SOLID WASTE

Solid waste can be classified into different types depending on their source:

(a) Household waste is generally classified as municipal waste,
(b) Industrial waste as hazardous waste, and
(c) Biomedical waste or hospital waste as infectious waste.

HOSPITAL WASTE

Hospital waste is generated during the diagnosis, treatment, or immunization of human beings or animals or in research activities in these fields or in the production or testing of biologicals. It may include wastes like sharps, soiled waste, disposables, anatomical waste, cultures, discarded medicines, chemical wastes, etc. These are in the form of disposable syringes, swabs, bandages, body fluids, human excreta, etc. This waste is highly infectious and can be a serious threat to human health if not managed in a scientific and discriminate manner. It has been roughly estimated that of the 4 kg of waste generated in a hospital at least 1 kg would be infected.

SOLID WASTES AND HEALTH HAZARD

Proper methods of waste disposal have to be undertaken to ensure that it does not affect the environment around the area or cause health hazards to the people living there.

At the household-level proper segregation of waste has to be done and it should be ensured that all organic matter is kept aside for composting, which is undoubtedly the best method for the correct disposal of this segment of the waste. In fact, the organic part of the waste that is generated decomposes more easily, attracts insects and causes disease. Organic waste can be composted and then used as a fertilizer.

ENVIRONMENTAL SANITATION

Latrines must be provided wherever large groups of people are living together. An education programme should be conducted to explain why and how the latrines should be used. Ideally, one latrine should be constructed for each family. Two common types of latrine are the ventilated improved pit (VIP) latrine (with vent pipe) and the pour-flush latrine (which is flushed by pouring into it about 3 litres of water after each defecation). Other types of latrine are described as follows:

Whenever latrines are provided, they should be:

(i) easy to reach at night;

(ii) cleaned at least daily (people will not use dirty latrines); staff may have to be employed for this;

(iii) sited well away from sources of drinking-water (at a distance of at least 30 metres) and 1.5-3 m above the water table).

Families should be instructed to keep latrines clean by regularly washing down dirty surfaces. If there are no latrines, defecation-fields should be organized as an emergency measure while the latrines are being built. These fields should be established at least 30 m away from any source of drinking-water. Families should be instructed to:

(i) defecate away from houses or shelters, paths, and areas where children play, and at least 30 m away from a water source;

(ii) avoid going barefoot to defecate;

(iii) prevent children from going to the defecation area alone.

The Deep-trench Latrine

The deep-trench latrine is designed for camps that are set up to last several months. It consists of a trench 2-4 m deep and 75-90 cm wide; its length depends on the number of users, but should provide 1 m for each place, and 1 place for every 4-5 people. A deep trench should be shored up to prevent collapse, and should be covered with a fly-proof floor made of strong pieces of wood or bamboo that overlap the edges of the trench by at least 50 cm. The floor should be plastered with mud, with holes of approximately 25 cm in diameter left at 1 metre intervals. (A reinforced concrete slab should be used, if possible.) Once the trench is filled to about 30 cm below ground-level, it should he filled in with earth and a new trench should be dug.

The Bore-hole Latrine

If the subsoil is not rocky and the water-table is very low (at least 7m below the ground-level), a hole can be made with an earth-auger; it should be about 40 cm in diameter and 5-6 m deep and should not penetrate the water-table. There should be one bore-hole latrine for every 20 people.

Septic Tanks

If the soil is sandy or very wet, trench latrines are impractical and septic tanks may have to be provided for drainage. These are normally drained by gravity, which makes it necessary to build an elevated Platform for latrines (or to site latrines on suitably sloping terrain). Septic tanks are widely available at relatively low cost; installation should be straightforward but expert advice may be needed. Equipment should be available for desludging the septic tanks regularly.

SANITATION AND HEALTH HAZARDS

A growing world population, unrelenting urbanization, increasing scarcity of good quality water resources and rising fertilizer prices are the driving forces behind the accelerating upward trend in the use of waste-water, excreta and grey-water for agriculture and aquaculture.

The health risks associated with this practice have been long recognized, but regulatory measures were, until recently, based on rigid guideline values whose application often was incompatible with the socio-economic settings where most waste-water use takes place.

The assessment of microbial hazards and toxic chemicals and the management of the associated risks when using waste-water and excreta in aquaculture. It explains requirements to promote safe use practices, including minimum procedures and specific health-based targets. It puts trade-offs between potential risks and nutritional benefits in a wider development context.

STUDY QUESTIONS

1. What do you mean by Environmental health?
2. Write short notes on the following:
   (a) Water-borne diseases;
   (b) Air-borne diseases; and
   (c) Sanitation and Health hazards.

■■■

7

FUNDAMENTALS OF MICROBIOLOGY

INTRODUCTION

Microbiology is the study of *micro-organisms*, which are unicellular or cell-cluster microscopic organisms. This includes eukaryotes such as fungi and protists, and prokaryotes, which are bacteria and archaea. Viruses, though not strictly classed as living organisms, are also studied. In short, microbiology refers to the study of life and organisms that are too small to be seen with the naked eye. Microbiology is a broad term which includes virology, mycology, parasitology, bacteriology and other branches. A microbiologist is a specialist in microbiology.

Microbiology is researched actively, and the field is advancing continually. We have probably only studied about one percent of all of the microbe species on Earth. Although microbes were first observed over three hundred years ago, the field of microbiology can be said to be in its infancy relative to older biological disciplines such as zoology and botany.

HISTORICAL DEVELOPMENT

Bacteria and micro-organisms were first observed by Antonie van Leeuwenhoek in 1676 using a single-lens microscope of his own design. In doing so Leeuwenhoek made one of the most important discoveries in biology and initiated the scientific fields of bacteriology and microbiology. Van Leeuwenhoek is often cited as the first microbiologist, the first recorded microbiological observation, that of the fruiting bodies of moulds, was made earlier in 1665 by Robert Hooke.

The field of bacteriology is generally considered to have been founded by *Ferdinand Cohn* (1828–1898), a botanist whose studies on algae and photosynthetic bacteria led him to describe several bacteria including Bacillus and Beggiatoa. Cohn was also the first to formulate a scheme for the taxonomic classification of bacteria. *Louis Pasteur* (1822–1895) and *Robert Koch* (1843–1910) were contemporaries of Cohn and are often considered to be the founders of medical microbiology. Pasteur is most famous for his series of experiments designed to disprove the then widely held theory of spontaneous generation, thereby solidifying microbiology's identity as a biological science.

Pasteur also designed methods for food preservation (pasteurization) and vaccines against several diseases such as anthrax, fowl cholera and rabies. Koch is best known for his contributions to the germ theory of disease, proving that specific diseases were caused by specific pathogenic micro-organisms. He developed a series of criteria that have become known as the Koch's postulates. Koch was one of the first scientists to focus on the isolation of bacteria in pure culture resulting in his description of several novel bacteria including Mycobacterium tuberculosis, the causative agent of tuberculosis.

While Pasteur and Koch are often considered the founders of microbiology, their work did not accurately reflect the true diversity of the microbial world because of their exclusive focus on micro-organisms having direct medical relevance. It was not until the work of *Martinus Beijerinck* (1851–1931) and Sergei Winogradsky (1856–1953), the founders of general microbiology (an older term encompassing aspects of microbial physiology, diversity and ecology), that the true breadth of microbiology was revealed. Beijerinck made two major contributions to microbiology: the discovery of viruses and the development of enrichment culture techniques. While his work on the Tobacco Mosaic Virus established the basic principles of virology, it was his development of enrichment culturing that had the most immediate impact on microbiology by allowing for the cultivation of a wide range of microbes with wildly different physiologies. Winogradsky was the first to develop the concept of chemo-lithotrophy and to thereby reveal the essential role played by micro-organisms in geochemical processes. He was responsible for the first isolation and description of both nitrifying and nitrogen-fixing bacteria.

CLASSIFICATION OF MICRO-ORGANISM

PROTISTS

Protists are a diverse group of eukaryotic micro-organisms. Historically, protists were treated as the kingdom Protista but this group is no longer recognized in modern taxonomy.The protists do not have much in common besides a relatively simple organization — either they are *unicellular*, or they are *multicellular* without specialized tissues. This simple cellular organization distinguishes the protists from other *eukaryotes*, such as fungi, animals and plants.

Protists were traditionally subdivided into several groups based on similarities to the "higher" kingdoms: the one-celled animal-like protozoa, the plant-like *protophyta* (mostly one-celled algae), and the fungus-like slime moulds and water moulds. Because these groups often overlap, they have been replaced by phylogenetic-based classifications. However, they are still useful as informal names for describing the morphology and ecology of protists.

PROKARYOTES AND EUKARYOTES

The *prokaryotes* are a group of organisms that lack a cell nucleus or any other membrane-bound organelles.

Animals, plants, fungi, and protists are *eukaryotes* organisms whose cells are organized into complex structures enclosed within membranes. The defining membrane-bound structure that differentiates eukaryotic cells from prokaryotic cells is the nucleus.

VIRUS

A virus (from the Latin virus meaning toxin or poison) is a sub-microscopic infectious agent that is unable to grow or reproduce outside a host cell. Viruses infect all cellular life. Viruses consist of two or three parts: all viruses have genes made from either DNA or RNA, long molecules that carry genetic information; all have a protein coat that protects these genes; and some have an envelope of fat that surrounds them when they are outside a cell. Viruses vary in shape from simple helical and icosahedral shapes, to more complex structures. They are about 100 times smaller than bacteria. The origins of viruses are unclear: some may have evolved from plasmids—pieces of DNA that can move between cells—while others may have evolved from bacteria.

Viruses spread in many ways; different species of virus use different methods. For example, plant viruses are often transmitted from plant to plant by insects that feed on sap, such as aphids, while animal viruses can be carried by blood-sucking insects. These disease-bearing organisms are known as vectors. Influenza viruses are spread by coughing and sneezing, and others such as norovirus are transmitted by the faecal-oral route, when they contaminate hands, food or water. Rotavirus is often spread by direct contact with infected children. HIV is one of several viruses that are transmitted through sex.

Not all viruses cause disease, as many viruses reproduce without causing any obvious harm to the infected organism. Some viruses such as HIV can cause life-long or chronic infections, and the viruses continue to replicate in the body despite the hosts' defence mechanisms. However, viral infections in animals usually cause an immune response, which can completely eliminate a virus. These immune responses can also be produced by vaccines that give lifelong immunity to a viral infection. Micro-organisms such as bacteria also have defences against viral infection, such as restriction modification systems. Antibiotics have no effect on viruses, but antiviral drugs have been developed to treat life-threatening infections.

BACTERIA

The bacteria are a large group of unicellular micro-organisms. Typically a few micrometres in length, bacteria have a wide range of shapes, ranging from spheres to rods and spirals. Bacteria are ubiquitous in every habitat on Earth, growing in soil, acidic hot springs, radioactive waste, water, and deep in the Earth's crust, as well as in organic matter and the live bodies of plants and animals. There are typically 40 million bacterial cells in a gram of soil and a million bacterial cells in a millilitre of fresh water; in all, there are approximately five million (5×1030) bacteria on Earth, forming much of the world's biomass. Bacteria are vital in recycling nutrients, with many important steps in nutrient cycles depending on these organisms, such as the fixation of nitrogen from the atmosphere and putrefaction. However, most bacteria have not been characterized, and only about half of the phyla of bacteria have species that can be cultured in the laboratory. The study of bacteria is known as *bacteriology*, a branch of *microbiology*.

BACTERIAL CELL STRUCTURE

INTRACELLULAR STRUCTURES

The bacterial cell is surrounded by a lipid membrane, or cell membrane, which encloses the contents of the cell and acts as a barrier to hold nutrients, proteins and other essential components of the cytoplasm within the cell. As they are prokaryotes, bacteria do not tend to have membrane-bound organelles in their cytoplasm and thus contain few large intracellular structures. They consequently lack a nucleus, mitochondria, chloroplasts and the other organelles present in eukaryotic cells, such as the Golgi apparatus and endoplasmic reticulum. Bacteria were once seen as simple bags of cytoplasm, but elements such as prokaryotic cytoskeleton, and the localization of proteins to specific locations within the cytoplasm have been found to show levels of complexity. These subcellular compartments have been called "bacterial hyperstructures".

Micro-compartments such as carboxysome provides a further level of organization, which are compartments within bacteria that are surrounded by polyhedral protein shells, rather than by lipid membranes. These "polyhedral organelles" localize and compartmentalize bacterial metabolism, a function performed by the membrane-bound organelles in eukaryotes.

EXTRACELLULAR STRUCTURES

Around the outside of the cell membrane is the bacterial cell wall. Bacterial cell walls are made of peptidoglycan (called murein in older sources), which is made from polysaccharide chains cross-linked by unusual peptides containing D-amino acids. Bacterial cell walls are different from the cell walls of plants and fungi, which are made of cellulose and chitin, respectively. The cell wall of bacteria is also distinct from that of Archaea, which do not contain peptidoglycan. The cell wall is essential to the survival of many bacteria, and the antibiotic penicillin is able to kill bacteria by inhibiting a step in the synthesis of peptidoglycan.

CLASSIFICATION OF BACTERIA ON THE BASIS OF GRAM STAINING

There are broadly speaking two different types of cell wall in bacteria, called ***Gram-positive*** and ***Gram-negative***. The names originate from the reaction of cells to the ***Gram stain***, a test long-employed for the classification of bacterial species.

Gram-positive bacteria are those that are stained dark blue or violet by Gram staining. This is in contrast to *Gram-negative bacteria,* which cannot retain the crystal violet stain, instead taking up the counterstain (safranin or fuchsin) and appearing red or pink. Gram-positive organisms are able to retain the crystal violet stain because of the high amount of peptidoglycan in the cell wall. Gram-positive cell walls typically lack the outer membrane found in Gram-negative bacteria.

Gram-positive bacteria possess a thick cell wall containing many layers of peptidoglycan and teichoic acids. In contrast, Gram-negative bacteria have a relatively thin cell wall consisting of a few layers of peptidoglycan surrounded by a second lipid membrane containing lipopolysaccharides and lipoproteins. Most bacteria have the Gram-negative cell wall, and only the Firmicutes and Actinobacteria (previously known as the low G+C and high G+C

Gram-positive bacteria, respectively) have the alternative Gram-positive arrangement. These differences in structure can produce differences in antibiotic susceptibility; for instance, vancomycin can kill only Gram-positive bacteria and is ineffective against Gram-negative pathogens, such as Haemophilus influenzae or Pseudomonas aeruginosa.

DIFFERENT TYPES OF BACTERIA

Bacteria are single-celled organisms, found in almost each and every type of environment. They are so small that they cannot be seen with the naked eye and have to be seen through a microscope. Infact, their size is measured in micro-metre (a millionth part of a metre). There are thousands of species of bacteria found in the world. However, we can classify these species into groups, depending upon a number of factors like their shape, gram strain, etc.

Classification on the Basis of Shapes

Bacteria are usually classified on the basis of their shapes. Broadly, they can be divided into

- Rod-shaped bacteria (Bacilli)
- Sphere-shaped bacteria (Cocci)
- Spiral-shaped bacteria (Spirilla).

Classification on the Basis of Gram Strain

This classification is based on the results of Gram Staining Method, in which an agent is used to bind to the cell wall of the bacteria.

- *Gram-positive*: Cocci, endospore-orming and nonsporing rods, mycobacteria, nonfilamentous actinomycetes.
- *Gram-negative*: Spirochetes, spiral and curved, aerobic and facultatively aerobic rods, obligate anaerobes, aerobic and anaerobic cocci, sulfate and sulfur-reducing, rickettsias, clamydias, mycoplasmas.

Classification on the Basis of Oxygen Requirement

This classification is based on the requirement of oxygen for the survival of the bacterium.

- Aerobic (Need Oxygen)
- Anaerobic (Do not need Oxygen).

Classification on the Basis of Growth and Reproduction

This classification is based on the growth and reproduction aspects of bacteria.

- Autotrophic Bacteria (Obtain carob and/or sugar from sunlight or chemical reactions)
- Heterotrophic Bacteria (Obtain carob and/or sugar from the environment).

Classification on the Basis of Phyla

This classification is based on the phyla, determined through morphology, DNA sequencing, conditions required and biochemistry, e.g., Aquificae, Bacteroids, Chlorobia, Chrysogenetic, Cyanobacteria, Fibrobacter, Firmicutes, Flavobacteria, Fuso-bacteria, Planctomycetes, Proteobacteria, Spirochaetes, Thermo-microbia, Verrucomicrobia, Xenobacteria.

PROTOZOAN CLASSIFICATION

Four major groups of protozoa are recognised and often given the status of phylum. Note, however, that in the animal kingdom proper (Metazoa), phyla are distinguished on their different body plans and that no comparable body plans are found in Protozoa. The groups are:

- Flagellates (or Mastigophora);
- Amoebae (or Sarcodina);
- Sporozoans (or Sporozoa, Apicomplexa); and
- Ciliates (or Ciliophora).

MORPHOLOGY OF FUNGI

Fungi are composed of filaments called ***hyphae***; their cells are long and thread-like and connected end-to-end, as you can see in the picture. Because of this diffuse association of their cells, the body of the organism is given the special name ***mycelium,*** a term which is applied to the whole body of any fungus. When reproductive hyphae are produced, they form a large organized

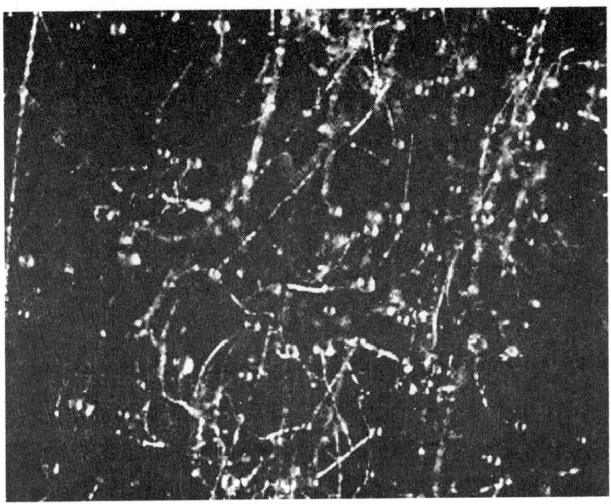

Fig. 7.1 *Fungi.*

structure called a ***sporocarp***, or ***mushroom*** or ***yeast***. This is produced solely for the release of spores, and is not the living, growing portion of the fungus.

In addition to being filamentous, fungal cells often have multiple nuclei. In the chytrids and zygomycetes, the cells are coenocytic, with no distinction between individual cells. Rather, the filaments are long and tubular, with a cytoplasm lining and large vacuole in the centre. By contrast, the ascomycetes and basidiomycetes are septate; their filaments are partitioned by cellular cross-walls called septa. The structure of these septa varies, and is taxonomically useful.

Another feature of fungi is the presence of chitin in their cell walls. This is a long carbohydrate polymer that also occurs in the exoskeletons of insects, spiders, and other arthropods. The chitin adds rigidity and structural support to the thin cells of the fungus, and makes fresh mushrooms crisp.

Most members of the Kingdom Fungi lack flagella; the structures are completely absent in all stages of their life cycle. The only exception are the chytrids, which produce flagellated gametes. The absence of flagella then, is a synapomorphy which unites all the remaining groups of fungi. This has had a tremendous impact on fungal biology, because it means that no fungus can produce motile gametes, and two organisms must therefore come into direct physical contact to effect sexual reproduction.

SYSTEMATIC CLASSIFICATION OF FUNGI

Fungi are usually classified in four divisions: the *Chytridiomycota* (chytrids), *Zygomycota* (bread molds), *Ascomycota* (yeasts and sac fungi), and the *Basidiomycota* (club fungi). Placement into a division is based on the way in which the fungus reproduces sexually. The shape and internal structure of the *sporangia,* which produce the spores, are the most useful character for identifying these various major groups.

There are also two conventional groups which are not recognized as formal taxonomic groups (i.e., they are polyphyletic); these are the *Deuteromycota* (fungi imperfecti), and the *lichens.*

The *Deuteromycota* includes all fungi which have lost the ability to reproduce sexually. As a result, it is not known for certain into which group they should be placed, and thus the Deuteromycota becomes a convenient place to dump them until someone gets around to working out their biology.

Unlike other fungi, the *lichens* are not a single organism, but rather a symbiotic association between a fungus and an alga. The fungal member of the lichen is usually an *ascomycete* or *basidiomycete,* and the *alga* is usually a *cyanobacterium* or a *chlorophyte* (green alga). Often the fungal partner is unable to grow without the algal symbiont, making it difficult to classify these organisms. They will be treated here as a separate group, but it should be realized that they are neither single organisms, nor a monophyletic group.

It should also be noted that some organisms carry the name of mould or fungus, but are *not* classified in the Kingdom Fungi. These include the *slime moulds* and *water moulds* (*Oomycota*). The slime moulds are now known to be a mixture of three or four unrelated groups, and the oomycetes are now classified in the *Chromista,* with the *diatoms* and *brown algae.*

VIRUSES

Viruses are infectious agents with both living and non-living characteristics.

1. Living Characteristics of Viruses

- They reproduce at a fantastic rate, but only in living host cells.
- They can mutate.

2. Nonliving Characteristics of Viruses

- They are acellular, that is, they contain no cytoplasm or cellular organelles.
- They carry out no metabolism on their own and must replicate using the host cell's metabolic machinery. In other words, viruses don't grow and divide. Instead, new viral components are synthesized and assembled within the infected host cell.
- The vast majority of viruses possess either DNA or RNA but not both.

Virus classification is currently based on five phenotypic characteristics; morphology, or structure, of the virus; type of nucleic acid, or the genetic material, of the virus; mode of replication; hosts; and the type of disease they cause. There are two classification systems in use today, the Baltimore system and the International Committee on the Taxonomy of Viruses classification guidelines.

The *seven groups* are: **Group I,** double stranded DNA viruses such as the herpes virus and the chickenpox virus; **Group II,** single stranded DNA viruses such as the parvo virus; **Group III,** double stranded RNA viruses; **Group IV,** positive-sense single stranded RNA viruses such as the Sars virus, the yellow fever virus and many other well known viruses; **Group V,** negative-sense single stranded RNA viruses such as the measles virus, the mumps virus and the rabies virus; **Group VI,** reverse transcribing RNA viruses such as HIV; and **Group VII,** reverse transcribing DNA viruses such as the hepatitis B virus.

The Group VI viruses use the enzyme to reverse-transcribe their RNA into DNA and then insert the transcribed DNA into the host organism's DNA, where it is replicated whenever a cell divides. The Group VII viruses transcribe their DNA into an RNA form, then transcribe the RNA back into DNA to be inserted into the host's DNA and replicated.

In the early 1990s, the International Committee on Taxonomy of Viruses devised and implemented rules for the naming and classification of viruses. This group still oversees the classification of viruses today. The ICTV system shares many features with the system used for classifying cellular organisms. There are several differences however; the classification of cellular organisms starts with the Kingdom, while viruses start with Order; another difference is the species name generally takes the form Disease species. For example the classification of the yellow fever virus is; Family - Flaviviridae, Genus - Flavivirus, Species - Yellow Fever virus. Notice this virus does not have an Order classification; that is because recognition of the Orders has been extremely slow, in over ten years only three Orders have been named. Many of the 80 known families remain unplaced. The ICTV are still working on this aspect of virus classification.

METHODS FOR CONTROLLING MICROBIAL GROWTH

Many methods to choose from:

PHYSICAL

- Heat (Dry, Moist, Pasteurization)
- Filtration
- Low Temperatures (fridge, freezer)
- Desication and osmotic pressure
- Radiation (ionizing and nonionizing).

CHEMICAL

- Phenol and phenolics
- Halogens
- Alcohol
- Heavy metals and their compounds
- Surface active agents (anionic and cationic detergents)
- Organic acids
- Gaseous sterilants

- Oxidising agents
- Chemotherapeutic agents target
    - cell wall
    - protein synthesis
    - nucleic acids
    - cell membrane
    - essential metabolites (antimetabolites).
- The method of choice depends on the situation and practicality of the approach.
- The material to be treated, e.g., heat labile or heat stable.
- Laboratory conditions differ from field conditions.
- Factors affecting growth, e.g., growing or resting cells, resistance factors.

FACTORS INFLUENCING THE EFFECTIVENESS OF CONTROL METHODS

A number of factors affect the usefulness (efficacy) of control methods and all factors should be considered to devise control measures.

SIZE OF MICROBIAL POPULATION

- Death is exponential ie more microbes = more time to kill the population
- Plot the log of the no. of surviving microbes vs time = straight line, the slope = killing rate
- Initial microbe concentrations one can predict the kill time.

EXPOSURE TIME OF THE AGENT

- Increasing exposure time increases kill rates; kill time used is usually well past the required minimal contact time
- Large volumes/vessels require more time for complete destruction.

EFFECT OF CONCENTRATION, TEMPERATURE AND pH

- Increasing concentration is similar to increasing exposure time
- Temperature, pH and concentration at which the agent works best

- Stability of the agent at various pHs and temperatures
- Legionella pnuemophila (Legionnaires disease) – the effect of the microbe suspended in tap water and exposed to different temperatures, pH and chlorine concentrations.

PROTECTIVE FEATURES OF THE MICROBES

- Endospore formers such as C. teta.
- Cysts – Protozoa
- Porins – Pseudomonas
- Cell wall – Mycobacterium tuberculosis (opportunistic pathogen)
- Active growth vs resting cells – antibiotics (penicillin - transpeptidase).

INTERACTIONS AND PROTECTIVE FEATURES AFFORDED BY THE ENVIRONMENT

- Sewage is rich in organics – polio virus protected
- Disinfecting in hospitals – selection of resistance
- Lipids and fats in dairy industry –protect spoilage microbes
- Remember that lab conditions used in testing are different to field conditions.

CONTROLLING MICROBIAL GROWTH IS NECESSARY

Decline in Salmonella typhi deaths in the US from 1 in 1000 (1900) to 4 in 200 million (1970) due to control measures:

- Water Chlorination (1908)
- Milk pasteurization (1909)
- Sewage treatment plant design improvements
- Transmission control
    - Fly populations (vectors)
    - Detection of diseased persons
        - carriers in the milk industry
        - patients
- Preventive vaccination
- Antibiotic therapy.

LISTER (1827-1912)

- Washing hands prior to surgery lead to decline in infection rates
- Heat sterilization of surgical instruments
- Application of phenol (carbolic acid) to wounds.

Todays control measures are more sophisticated and include a wide array of methods but not all methods do not kill microbes, e.g., filtration = removal.

STUDY QUESTIONS

1. What do you mean by Micro-organism?
2. Explain the structure of Bacterial Cell.
3. Discuss the Systematic classification of Fungi.

■■■

8

Communicable Diseases

COMMUNICABLE DISEASES

A communicable disease is a disease/illness that can be passed from one host to another (i.e., a host may be human or non-human). An infectious illness may be due to different germs such as bacteria, viruses and fungi. These germs survive on hands and objects such as taps, toys and bench tops. The length of time a germ survives on a surface will depend on the characteristics of the germ itself, the surface it has contaminated and how often that surface has been cleaned. Washing with detergent or soap and water is a very effective way of removing germs.

TRANSMISSION OF COMMUNICABLE DISEASE

Transmission of an infectious disease may occur through one or more of diverse pathways, including physical contact with infected individuals. These infecting agents may also be transmitted through liquids, food, body fluids, contaminated objects, air-borne inhalation, or through vector-borne spread.Communicable diseases are usually transmitted in one of five ways:

VECTORS

Infected mosquitoes, mites, flies and other insects can transmit disease to humans through their bites or by contaminating food and water. Examples include Ross River virus, scrub typhus, dengue fever and gastrointestinal illness.

CONTACT

Some diseases are transmitted from person to person by direct contact eg. school sores, conjunctivitis, sexually transmitted diseases can be spread through lack of personal protective measures during sex. *Direct contact transmission* involves immediate contact between two people (or with an animal). *Indirect contact transmission* involves fomites; an object that becomes contaminated by touch (the fomite) then spreads the infection by touch.

Most germs have to enter the mouth, nose, or eye to cause an infection, but there are several that can spread directly from skin to skin.

Skin-to-skin transmission occurs when bacteria, viruses, or parasites found on the skin of one child (or animal) are "caught" by another child through touch.

Bacterial infections, such as the staph or strep that cause the rash of impetigo, usually spread only if there is a break in the skin, perhaps from an insect bite, a scratch, or repeatedly wiping the irritated skin under an ongoing runny nose. The same tends to be true for viral infections, such as herpes simplex.

Superficial fungal or yeast infections might spread in the absence of a break in the skin—especially where the skin is warm, moist, and dark.

Parasites such as scabies or lice travel from child to child with ease. Sometimes they stop on a hairbrush or hat along the way.

How can it be prevented

When practical, avoiding direct contact with infected children is the general key—especially when there is a break in the skin. In addition, hand cleansing and surface disinfecting can interrupt some disease transmission. Also, it is generally wise for children to avoid sharing hairbrushes, combs, and hats.

Spread from faeces to mouths

Gastrointestinal illness is caused by bacteria, viruses or parasites. It often occurs when germs from the faeces get on to someone's hands and then into someone else's mouth, e.g., salmonella, hepatitis A.

Contact with body secretions or blood

Direct contact with blood can cause spread of infection eg. hepatitis B. Other body fluids like urine can also be infectious.

AIR-BORNE

Air-borne transmission occurs when *bacteria* or *viruses* travel on *dust* particles or on small respiratory *droplets* that may become aerosolized when people sneeze, cough, laugh, or exhale. They hang in the air much like invisible smoke. They can travel on air currents over considerable distances. These droplets are loaded with infectious particles.

Coughing and sneezing by an infectious person disperses infectious droplets into the atmosphere which are in turn inhaled by others. Examples of respiratory diseases include the common cold, influenza, chicken pox, measles and whooping cough (pertussis). With air-borne transmission, direct contact with someone who is infected is not necessary to become ill. The amount of exposure necessarily varies from disease to disease. With chickenpox, a child could easily catch it from another aisle in a supermarket. With tuberculosis, closer contact and less air circulation are often needed.

Many common infections can spread by air-borne transmission at least in some cases, including:

- Anthrax (inhalational)
- Chickenpox
- Influenza
- Smallpox
- Tuberculosis.

How can it be prevented

The best way to avoid air-borne infections is to be in a different room from the person who is ill, with a closed door in between. If you need to be in the same room, wearing a mask may help for a brief exposure. Covering the mouth or nose when coughing or sneezing decreases droplet spread some.

DROPLET

Droplet transmission occurs when bacteria or viruses travel on relatively large respiratory droplets that people sneeze, cough, drip, or exhale. They travel only short distances before settling, usually less than 3 feet. These droplets are loaded with infectious particles.

They can be spread directly if people are close enough to each other. More often, though, fomites are involved. The droplets land on hands, toys, tables, mats, or other surfaces, where they sometimes remain infectious for hours. Hands that come in contact with these surfaces (doorknobs, telephones, pens, etc.) become contagious. When the infectious hand touches the nose or eyes, the infection is able to enter the new person.

Many common infections can spread by droplet transmission in at least some cases, including:

- Common cold
- Diptheria
- Fifth disease (erythema infectiosum)
- Influenza
- Meningitis
- Mycoplasma
- Mumps
- Pertussis (whooping cough)
- Plague
- Rubella
- Strep (strep throat, scarlet fever, pneumonia).

How can it be prevented

Frequent hand cleansing, especially with instant hand sanitizers, can help prevent droplet transmission. Hand cleansing is most important before eating and before touching the nose or eyes.

Covering the mouth or nose when coughing or sneezing decreases droplet spread—and makes hand cleansing even more important.

Using disposable towels and cups reduces the risk for infection. Cleaning or disinfecting commonly touched infected surfaces (doorknobs, faucet handles, shared toys, mats in daycare) can also help. Wearing a mask may help for brief, short exposures.

FAECAL–ORAL TRANSMISSION

Faecal–oral transmission occurs when bacteria or viruses found in the stool of one child (or animal) are swallowed by another child. This is especially common in group-daycare settings, where faecal organisms are commonly found on surfaces and on the hands of providers. Usually, the contamination is invisible.

With some infections, such as rotavirus, only a few viral particles are needed to cause an infection. These can spread directly through a group-care setting quite quickly, often spreading by fomites. Other infections, such as salmonella, require a larger number of organisms to establish an infection. In the absence of visible stool contamination, these infections often travel through infected food or beverages.

Swimming pools and water parks can also be locations of faecal–oral transmission. If the water is not visibly contaminated and is adequately chlorinated, just getting the water in the mouth is usually not enough to cause an infection; the risk is greatly increased by swallowing.

Many common infections can spread by faecal–oral transmission in at least some cases, including:

- Adenovirus
- Campylobacter infection
- Coxsackievirus (hand-foot-mouth disease)

- Enteroviruses
- *E. coli* infection
- Giardia infection
- Hepatitis A virus
- Pinworms
- Polio
- Rotavirus
- Salmonella
- Tapeworms

How can it be prevented

Frequent hand cleansing, especially with instant hand sanitizers, is the most significant step to help prevent faecal–oral transmission. Hand cleansing is most important after toileting or diapering and before eating.

- Safe and careful food-handling practices are also vital.
- Teach children never to swallow water in pools or water-play areas.

In daycare settings, the fewer children in diapers or under age 3, the smaller the risk for faecal–oral transmission of infections. Diaper-changing surfaces should never be close to food-preparation areas and should be sanitized between uses. Soiled diapers need to be properly disposed of.

Using disposable towels and cups reduces the risk for infection. Cleaning or disinfecting commonly touched, infected surfaces (doorknobs, faucet handles, shared toys, sleep mats) can also help.

WATER-BORNE TRANSMISSION

Water-borne transmission allows diarrheal pathogens to be transported from immobilized infected hosts to uninfected hosts. Where water supplies are not protected, a person with incapacitating diarrheal illness will release the diarrheal pathogens into clothes, bed sheets, or containers for collecting excreta. These items then tend to be removed by attendants and washed in bodies of water such as canals or rivers, which may be used as sources of drinking water or may flow into supplies of drinking water. Either way, the cycle is completed when susceptible individuals drink the contaminated water. In this situation, highly exploitative (and hence highly virulent) pathogen variants should be favoured by natural selection because the benefits of intense exploitation are great and the costs of exploitation are small. The benefits are great because large numbers of susceptibles can be infected by the increased numbers of propagules in the water. The costs are low because the incapacitating illness associated with this propagule production should have relatively little negative effect on the water-borne transmission of the propagules–rather than relying on the mobility of the infected individuals to enact transmission, the pathogens are using the mobility of the attendants and the water.

INSECT-BORNE TRANSMISSION

Typhoid Fever

Typhoid fever is a bacterial disease, caused by *Salmonella typhi*. It is transmitted through the ingestion of food or drink contaminated by the faeces or urine of infected people.

Symptoms usually develop 1–3 weeks after exposure, and may be mild or severe. They include high fever, malaise, headache, constipation or diarrhoea, rose-coloured spots on the chest, and enlarged spleen and liver. Healthy carrier state may follow acute illness.

Typhoid fever can be treated with antibiotics. However, resistance to common antimicrobials is widespread. Healthy carriers should be excluded from handling food.

MALARIA

Malaria is caused by a parasite called Plasmodium, which is transmitted via the bites of infected mosquitoes. In the human body, the parasites multiply in the liver, and then infect red blood cells.

Symptoms of malaria include fever, headache, and vomiting, and usually appear between 10 and 15 days after the mosquito bite. If not treated, malaria can quickly become life-threatening by disrupting the blood supply to vital organs. In many parts of the world, the parasites have developed resistance to a number of malaria medicines.

Key interventions to control malaria include: prompt and effective treatment with artemisinin-based combination therapies; use of insecticidal nets by people at risk; and indoor residual spraying with insecticide to control the vector mosquitoes.

PLACENTAL TRANSMISSION

Measles (also known as *rubeola*) is a disease caused by a virus, specifically a paramyxovirus of the genus Morbillivirus. Symptoms include fever, cough, runny nose, red eyes and a generalized, maculopapular, erythematous rash.

Measles is spread through respiration (contact with fluids from an infected person's nose and mouth, either directly or through aerosol transmission), and is highly contagious—90% of people without immunity sharing a house with an infected person will catch it. Airborne precautions should be taken for all suspected cases of measles. The incubation period usually lasts for 4–12 days (during which there are no symptoms). Infected people remain contagious from the appearance of the first symptoms until 3–5 days after the rash appears.

'German measles' is an unrelated condition caused by the rubella virus. The classical symptoms of measles include a three-day fever, the three Cs—cough, coryza (runny nose) and conjunctivitis (red eyes). The fever may reach up to 40° Celsius (104° Fahrenheit). Koplik's spots seen inside the mouth are pathognomonic (diagnostic) for measles but are not often seen, even in real cases of measles, because they are transient and may disappear within a day of arising.

The characteristic measles rash is classically described as a generalized, maculopapular, erythematous rash that begins several days after the fever starts. It starts on the head before spreading to cover most of the body, often causing itching. The rash is said to "stain", changing colour from red to dark brown, before disappearing.

Syphilis

Syphilis is a sexually transmitted disease caused by the spirochetal bacterium Treponema pallidum subspecies pallidum. The route of transmission of syphilis is almost always through sexual contact, although there are examples of congenital syphilis via transmission from mother to child in utero.

The signs and symptoms of syphilis are numerous; before the advent of serological testing, precise diagnosis was very difficult. In fact, the disease was dubbed the "Great Imitator" because it was often confused with other diseases, particularly in its tertiary stage.

Syphilis can generally be treated with antibiotics, including penicillin. One of the oldest and still the most effective method is an intramuscular injection of benzathine penicillin. If left untreated, syphilis can damage the heart, aorta, brain, eyes, and bones. In some cases these effects can be fatal. In 1998, the complete genetic sequence of *T. pallidum* was published, which may aid understanding of the pathogenesis of syphilis.

OTHERS COMMUNICABLE DISEASES

DIPTHERIA

Diptheria is a bacterial infection that spreads easily and occurs quickly. It mainly affects the nose and throat. Children under 5 and adults over 60 years old are particularly at risk for contracting the infection. People living in crowded or unclean conditions, those who aren't well nourished, and children and adults who don't have up-to-date immunizations are also at risk.

Signs and Symptoms

In its early stages, diptheriacan be mistaken for a bad sore throat. A low-grade fever and swollen neck glands are the other early symptoms.

The toxin, or poison, caused by the bacteria can lead to a thick coating in the nose, throat, or airway. This coating is usually fuzzy gray or black and can cause breathing problems and difficulty in swallowing. The formation of this coating (or membrane) in the nose, throat, or airway makes a diptheria infection different from other more common infections (such as strep throat) that cause sore throat.

As the infection progresses, the person may:

- have difficulty breathing or swallowing
- complain of double vision
- have slurred speech
- even show signs of going into shock (skin that's pale and cold, rapid heartbeat, sweating, and an anxious appearance).

In cases that progress beyond a throat infection, diptheria toxin spreads through the bloodstream and can lead to potentially life-threatening complications that affect other organs of the body, such as the heart and kidneys. The toxin can cause damage to the heart that affects its ability to pump blood or the kidneys' ability to clear wastes. It can also cause nerve damage, eventually leading to paralysis. Up to 40% to 50% of those who don't get treated can die.

Prevention

Preventing diptheria depends almost completely on immunizing children with the diptheria/tetanus/pertussis (DTP or DTaP) vaccine and non-immunized adults with the diptheria/tetanus vaccine (DT). Most cases of diptheriaoccur in people who haven't received the vaccine at all or haven't received the entire course.

SMALLPOX

Smallpox is a very serious illness caused by a virus called the variola virus. Smallpox gets its name from the pus-filled blisters (or pocks) that form during the illness. Although the names may sound alike, smallpox is not related to chickenpox, which is a milder disease caused by a different virus.

Smallpox spreads very easily from person to person. Symptoms are flu-like and include high fever, fatigue and headache and backache, followed by a rash with flat red sores.

Smallpox is contagious. That means the virus can spread to others. It spreads through tiny drops of the infected person's saliva (spit) when the person coughs, talks, or sneezes. Smallpox usually passes from person to person during close, face-to-face contact.

If someone does get smallpox, a doctor can recognize the disease because it causes a special kind of rash. The rash shows up as blisters on the skin that fill with fluid and crust over. This may sound like chickenpox, but the blisters look different from the blisters that chickenpox causes. The other symptoms of smallpox are like those of many other less serious illnesses: fever, headache, backache, and feeling tired.

INFLUENZA

Influenza, commonly called "the flu," is an illness caused by viruses that infect the respiratory tract. Compared with most other viral respiratory infections, such as the common cold, influenza (flu) infection often causes a more severe illness with a mortality rate (death rate) of about 0.1% of people who are infected with the virus.

Haemophilus influenzae is a bacterium that causes lung infections in infants and children, and it occasionally causes ear, eye, sinus, joint, and a few other infections, but not the flu. Typical clinical features of influenza include:

- fever (usually 100°F to 103°F in adults and often even higher in children),
- respiratory symptoms such as
- cough,
- sore throat,
- runny or stuffy nose,
- headache,
- muscle aches, and
- fatigue, sometimes extreme.

Although nausea, vomiting, and diarrhea can sometimes accompany influenza infection, especially in children, gastro-intestinal symptoms are rarely prominent. The term "stomach flu" is a misnomer that is sometimes used to describe gastrointestinal illnesses caused by other microorganisms.

BIRD FLU

The bird flu, also known as avian influenza, is an infection caused by avian influenza A. Bird flu can infect many bird species, including domesticated birds such as chickens. In most cases, the disease is mild; however, some subtypes can be pathogenic and rapidly kill birds within 48 hours. Rarely, humans can be infected by these bird viruses. People who get infected with bird flu usually have direct contact with the infected birds or their waste products. Depending on the viral type, the infections can range from mild influenza to severe respiratory problems or death.

Prevention

Vaccination is the primary method for control of influenza; however, antiviral agents have a role in the prevention and treatment of mainly influenza type A infection. Regardless, antiviral agents should not be considered as a substitute or alternative for vaccination.

CHICKENPOX

Chickenpox is a common illness among kids, particularly those under age 12. An itchy rash of spots that look like blisters can appear all over the body and may be accompanied by flu-like symptoms. Symptoms usually go away without treatment, but because the infection is very contagious, an infected child should stay home and rest until the symptoms are gone.

Chickenpox is caused by the varicella-zoster virus (VZV). Kids can be protected from VZV by getting the chickenpox (varicella) vaccine, usually between the ages of 12 and 15 months.

A person usually has only one episode of chickenpox, but VZV can lie dormant within the body and cause a different type of skin eruption later in life called shingles (or herpes zoster). Getting the chickenpox vaccine significantly lowers your child's chances of getting chickenpox, but he or she may still develop shingles later.

Symptoms of Chickenpox

Chickenpox causes a red, itchy rash on the skin that usually appears first on the abdomen or back and face, and then spreads to almost everywhere else on the body, including the scalp, mouth, nose, ears, and genitals.

The rash begins as multiple small, red bumps that look like pimples or insect bites. They develop into thin-walled blisters filled with clear fluid, which becomes cloudy. The blister wall breaks, leaving open sores, which finally crust over to become dry, brown scabs.

Chickenpox blisters are usually less than a quarter of an inch wide, have a reddish base, and appear in bouts over 2 to 4 days. The rash may be more extensive or severe in kids who have skin disorders such as eczema.

Some kids have a fever, abdominal pain, sore throat, headache, or a vague sick feeling a day or 2 before the rash appears. These symptoms may last for a few days, and fever stays in the range of 100°–102° Fahrenheit (37.7°–38.8°C), though in rare cases may be higher. Younger kids often have milder symptoms and fewer blisters than older children or adults.

MEASLES

Measles, also called *rubeola,* is a highly contagious respiratory infection that's caused by a virus. It causes a total-body skin rash and flu-like symptoms, including a fever, cough, and runny nose.

Signs and Symptoms

While measles is probably best known for the full-body rash it causes, the first symptoms of the infection are usually a hacking cough, runny nose, high fever, and red eyes. A characteristic marker of measles are Koplik's spots, small red spots with blue-white centres that appear inside the mouth.

The measles rash typically has a red or reddish brown blotchy appearance, and first usually shows up on the forehead, then spreads downward over the face, neck, and body, then down to the arms and feet.

MUMPS

Mumps is a disease caused by a virus that usually spreads through saliva and can infect many parts of the body, especially the parotid salivary glands. These glands, which produce saliva for the mouth, are found toward the back of each cheek, in the area between the ear and jaw. In cases of mumps, these glands typically swell and become painful.

Signs and Symptoms

Cases of mumps may start with a fever of up to 103°Fahrenheit (39.4°C), as well as a headache and loss of appetite. The well-known hallmark of mumps is swelling and pain in the parotid glands, making the child look like a hamster with food in its cheeks. The glands usually become increasingly swollen and painful over a period of 1 to 3 days. The pain gets worse when the child swallows, talks, chews, or drinks acidic juices (like orange juice).

Both the left and right parotid glands may be affected, with one side swelling a few days before the other, or only one side may swell. In rare cases, mumps will attack other groups of salivary glands instead of the parotids. If this happens, swelling may be noticed under the tongue, under the jaw, or all the way down to the front of the chest.

Mumps can lead to inflammation and swelling of the brain and other organs, although this is not common. Encephalitis (inflammation of the brain) and meningitis (inflammation of the lining of the brain and spinal cord) are both rare complications of mumps. Symptoms appear in the first week after the parotid glands begin to swell and may include: high fever, stiff neck, headache, nausea and vomiting, drowsiness, convulsions, and other signs of brain involvement.

Mumps in adolescent and adult males may also result in the development of orchitis, an inflammation of the testicles. Usually one testicle becomes swollen and painful about 7 to 10 days after the parotids swell. This is accompanied by a high fever, shaking chills, headache, nausea, vomiting, and abdominal pain that can sometimes be mistaken for appendicitis if the right testicle is affected.

After 3 to 7 days, testicular pain and swelling subside, usually at about the same time that the fever passes. In some cases, both testicles are involved. Even with involvement of both testicles, sterility is only a rare complication of orchitis.

Additionally, mumps may affect the pancreas or, in females, the ovaries, causing pain and tenderness in parts of the abdomen.

In some cases, signs and symptoms are so mild that no one suspects a mumps infection. Doctors believe that about 1 in 3 people may have a mumps infection without symptoms.

DIARRHOEA

Diarrhoea is also called *loose motions*. Diarrhoea is not itself a disease, but can be a symptom of several diseases. Diarrhoea means there are frequent, loose or liquid stools. There may be abdominal pain, which may reduce after a stool is passed. Acute diarrhoea may come on suddenly for a short time. Chronic diarrhoea may affect someone for a long period of time. If you have diarrhoea for long periods of time, it may be very troubling and you may feel very weak and tired.

Diarrhoea causes dehydration. Children are more likely than adults to die from diarrhoea because they become dehydrated more quickly. Diarrhoea is also a major cause of child malnutrition.

Symptoms

Frequent, loose, watery stools, loss of appetite, nausea, vomiting, stomach pains, fever, abdominal pain, abdominal cramps, dehydration, pricking sensation.Sometimes bacterial or parasitic infections sometimes cause bloody stools.

Diarrhoea may also be caused due to a chronic problem like viral stomach flu. Diarrhoea occurs when the lining of the small or large intestine is irritated. It leads to increased water being passed in the stools. The causes of diarrhoea are many. Out of which the main causes are listed below:

Bacterial infections: Several types of bacteria which get into our body through contaminated food or water, are the main causes of diarrhea.

Viral infections: Many viruses are also responsible for the cause of diarrhea, including rotavirus, Norwalk virus, cytomegalovirus, herpes simplex virus, and viral hepatitis.

Parasitic infections are also a cause for diarrhoea.

Food Intolerance: Some people are not able to digest some component of food properly, such as lactose, the sugar found in milk — which ultimately leads to diarrhoea.

CHOLERA

Cholera is an acute intestinal infection caused by ingestion of food or water contaminated by a comma-shaped bacteria Vibrio cholerae, the most feared epidemic diarrhoeal disease because of its severity.

Signs and Symptoms of Cholera

Symptoms begin 1 to 3 days after infection and range from mild, uncomplicated diarrhea to severe, potentially fatal disease. Some infected people have no symptoms. The infection is often mild or without symptoms, but sometimes can be severe. The infected person has several symptoms which can be characterized by:

- Abdominal cramps
- Dehydration
- Diarrhoea has a "fishy" odour
- Dry mouth
- Dry skin
- Excessive thirst
- Leg cramps
- Low urine output
- Low blood pressure
- Nausea
- Rapid heart rate
- Sunken eyes
- Tiredness
- Unusual sleepiness

- Vomiting
- Watery diarrhoea.

In the infected persons, rapid loss of body fluids leads to dehydration and shock. Without treatment, death can occur within hours.

Preventions of Cholera

Cholera is usually transmitted through contaminated water or food. Outbreaks can occur in any part of the world where water supply, sanitation, food safety, and hygiene are inadequate.

- Drink only boiled water or water that has been treated with chlorine or iodine.
- Eat only thoroughly cooked food and are still hot, or fruit that you have peeled yourself.
- Avoid undercooked or raw fish or shellfish.
- Make sure all vegetables are cooked properly, avoid salads.
- Avoid foods and beverages from street vendors.
- Do not bring perishable seafood.
- Check for proper sanitation and water purification systems.
- Give liquid bland foods, lemon, onions and mint to the patient.
- Vegetables and fruits must be washed with solution of potassium permanganate.
- New vaccines for cholera are available and appear to provide a somewhat better immunity and fewer side-effects than the previously available vaccine.

Health education aimed at behaviour change is thus an important component of cholera prevention and control.

Jaundice is a yellowing of the skin and the whites of the eyes caused by an accumulation of a cellular waste production called bilirubin. The discoloration is often, but by no means always, accompanied by itching, which can be intense, as well as by nausea, vomiting, headache, fever, dark-colored urine, abdominal pain, loss of appetite, abdominal swelling, and light-colored stools.

JAUNDICE

Jaundice is not a disease in and of itself, but a sign that the liver is having a problem handling bilirubin as it should. The liver makes bilirubin from dying red blood cells and other sources. It then converts bilirubin into bile, which has several purposes, among them the digestion of fatty acids and neutralization of stomach acid. If there is too much bilirubin for the liver to deal with, or if the liver's functioning is compromised, jaundice can result.

The specific causes of jaundice are numerous. The major categories of problems that can lead to jaundice include conditions that result in an excessive breakdown of red blood cells; hereditary disease that impair the liver's ability to convert bilirubin into bile; liver damage from exposure to toxic chemicals, including alcohol, carbon tetrachloride, and others; liver diseases such as hepatitis, bacterial infection, parasitic infestation, or cancer; and obstructions that block the outflow of bile so that it cannot leave the liver as it is supposed to. Newborns often develop some degree of jaundice in the days after birth, as their bodies adjust to life outside the womb, but this is not usually a serious problem.

ROUNDWORM INFECTIONS

Roundworm infections are diseases of the digestive tract and other organ systems caused by nematodes. Nematodes are parasitic worms with long, cylindrical bodies.

Roundworm infections are widespread throughout the world, with some regional differences. Ascariasis and trichuriasis are more common in warm, moist climates where people use human or animal faeces for fertilizer.

Causes and Symptoms

The causes and symptoms of roundworm infection vary according to the species. Humans acquire most types of roundworm infection from contaminated food or by touching the mouth with unwashed hands.

Ascariasis, which is caused by Ascaris lumbricoides, is one of the most widespread parasitic infections in humans, affecting over

1.3 billion people worldwide. Ascarid roundworms cause a larger burden on the human host than any other parasite; adult worms can grow as long as 12 or 14 inches, and release 200,000 eggs per day. The eggs infect people who eat unwashed vegetables from contaminated soil or touch their mouths with unwashed hands. Once inside the digestive tract, the eggs release larvae that penetrate the intestinal wall and migrate to the lungs through the liver and the bloodstream. After about 10 days in the lungs, the larvae migrate further into the patient's upper lung passages and airway, where they are swallowed. When they return to the intestine, they mature into adults and reproduce. The time period from the beginning of the infection to egg production is 60-75 days.

Prevention

There are no effective vaccines against any of the soil-transmitted roundworms, nor does infection confer immunity. Prevention of infection or reinfection requires adequate hygiene and sanitation measures, including regular and careful hand-washing before eating or touching the mouth with the hands.

With respect to specific infections, anisakiasis can be prevented by avoiding raw or improperly prepared fish or squid. Trichuriasis, ascariasis, and toxocariasis can be prevented by keeping children from playing in soil contaminated by human or animal faeces; by teaching children to wash their hands before eating; and by having pets dewormed regularly by a veterinarian.

THREADWORM INFECTION

Threadworm infection is an intestinal disease, which occasionally spreads to the skin, caused by a type of parasitic roundworm (helminth). In untreated patients, the disease has a high rate of reinfection caused by worms already present in the body. This type of disease recurrence is called *autoinfection*. Because of autoinfection, threadworms can remain inside humans for as long as 45 years after the initial infestation.

Human beings are universally susceptible to threadworm infection, although adults and older children are at greater risk of infection than younger children. The disease does not confer immunity. In addition to humans, threadworms can infect dogs, cats, horses, pigs, rats, and monkeys.

The infection is most commonly transmitted when a person comes into contact—usually by walking barefoot—with soil containing *S. stercoralis* larvae in their filariform stage. The threadlike larvae penetrate the skin, enter the lymphatic system, and are carried by the blood to the lungs. Once in the lungs, the larvae burst out of the capillaries into the patient's main respiratory system. They migrate upwards—usually without symptoms—to the patient's throat, where they are swallowed and carried down into the digestive tract. The filariform larvae settle in the small intestine. They mature into adults that deposit eggs that hatch—usually in the intestines—into noninfectious rhabdoid larvae. The rhabdoid larvae then migrate into the patient's large intestine and are excreted in the faeces. The time from initial penetration of the skin to excretion is 17-28 days. The rhabdoid larvae metamorphose into the infective filariform stage in the soil.

Threadworms are unique among human parasites in having both free-living and parasitic forms. In the free-living life cycle, some rhabdoid larvae develop into adult worms that live in contaminated soil and produce eggs that hatch into new rhabdoid larvae. The adult worms may live as long as five years.

Signs and Symptoms

The signs and symptoms of threadworm infection vary according to the stage of the disease as the larvae migrate throughout the body. Patients who suffer from autoinfection may have chronic or intermittent symptoms for years after they are first infected.

Prevention

There is no effective immunization against threadworm infection. Prevention of the disease requires careful attention to personal and institutional hygiene in endemic areas, including handwashing after defecating and before handling food. Other precautions include wearing shoes when visiting countries with high rates of threadworm infection, and monitoring close contacts of patients for signs of infection.

TAPEWORM INFECTION

Tapeworm infection usually occurs when you eat food or drink water contaminated with tapeworm eggs or larvae. Most people infected with tapeworm are unaware they're carrying them. Tapeworms occur in humans in one of two forms. If ingested as eggs, they may develop into larvae that migrate out of the intestines and form cysts in other tissues such as the lungs or liver. These cysts can cause serious problems. Or, if ingested as larvae, they typically develop into adult tapeworms in the intestines, which usually cause few or no symptoms.

A tapeworm infection that's confined to your intestines is easily treated with oral medications, and the prognosis for eradication is good. However, when the disease has migrated to other parts of your body, treatment is more difficult and untreated cases can be life-threatening.

Signs and Symptoms of Intestinal Infection

Most likely, you won't have any signs or symptoms with an intestinal infection. It is possible you might notice segments of the adult tapeworm (proglottids) in your stool. Other possible signs and symptoms include:

- Nausea
- Weakness
- Loss of appetite
- Abdominal pain
- Diarrhoea.
- Weight loss and inadequate absorption of nutrients from food.

Signs and Symptoms of Invasive Infection

If tapeworm larvae have moved out of your intestines and formed cysts in other tissues, it can cause organ and tissue damage, resulting in:

- Fever
- Cystic masses or lumps
- Allergic reactions to the larvae
- Bacterial infections
- Neurological symptoms or seizures if the brain is involved.

Prevention

To prevent tapeworm infection:

- Wash your hands with soap and water before eating or handling food and after using the toilet.
- When travelling in areas where tapeworm is found, wash and cook all fruits and vegetables with safe water before eating.
- Eliminate livestock exposure to tapeworm eggs by properly disposing of animal and human faeces.
- Thoroughly cook meat at temperatures of at least 150°F (66°C) to kill tapeworm eggs or larvae.
- Freeze meat for at least 12 hours and fish for at least 24 hours to kill tapeworm eggs and larvae.
- Avoid eating raw or undercooked pork, beef and fish.

SCABIES

Scabies is an infestation by the itch mite, Sarcoptes scabiei. Mites are small eight-legged parasites (in contrast to insects, which have six legs). They are tiny, just 1/3 millimetre long, and burrow into the skin to produce intense itching, which tends to be worse at night. The mites which cause scabies are not visible with the naked eye but can be seen with a magnifying glass or microscope.

Scabies mites are very sensitive to their environment. They can only live off of a host body for 24 to 36 hours under most conditions. Transmission of the mites involves close person-to-person contact of the skin-to-skin variety. It is hard, if not impossible, to catch scabies by shaking hands, hanging your coat next to someone who has it, or even sharing bedclothes that had mites in them the night before. The physical contact required to contract scabies may, however, be sexual, and sexual contact is the most common form of transmission among sexually active young people. However, other forms of physical contact, such as mothers hugging their children, is sufficient to spread the mites. Over time, close friends and relatives can contract it this way, too. School settings typically do not provide the level of close personal contact necessary for transmission of the mites.

SEXUALLY TRANSMITTED DISEASE

A sexually transmitted disease (STD) or venereal disease (VD), is an illness that has a significant probability of transmission between humans or animals by means of sexual contact, including vaginal intercourse, oral sex, and anal sex. Increasingly, the term sexually transmitted infection (STI) is used, as it has a broader range of meaning; a person may be infected, and may potentially infect others, without showing signs of disease. Some STIs can also be transmitted via use of an IV drug needle after its use by an infected person, as well as through childbirth or breastfeeding.

Syphilis is a sexually transmitted disease caused by the spirochetal bacterium Treponema pallidum subspecies pallidum. The route of transmission of syphilis is almost always through sexual contact, although there are examples of congenital syphilis via transmission from mother to child in utero.

Gonorrhea (also gonorrhoea), caused by the bacteria Neisseria gonorrhoeae, is a common sexually transmitted infection. Gonorrhea typically spreads during sexual intercourse. It can also be vertically transmitted, where infected mothers can pass gonorrhea to their newborn infants during delivery. This causes conjunctivitis (eye infections) which, if left untreated, can lead to blindness.

Chancroid is a sexually transmitted infection characterized by painful sores on the genitalia. Chancroid is known to be spread from one to another individual through sexual contact.

Candidiasis, commonly called yeast infection or thrush, is a fungal infection (mycosis) of any of the Candida species, of which Candida albicans is the most common.

Human immunodeficiency virus (HIV) is a lentivirus (a member of the retrovirus family) that can lead to acquired immunodeficiency syndrome (AIDS), a condition in humans in which the immune system begins to fail, leading to life-threatening opportunistic infections. Previous names for the virus include human T-lymphotropic virus-III (HTLV-III), lymphadenopathy-associated virus (LAV), and AIDS-associated retrovirus (ARV).

Infection with HIV occurs by the transfer of blood, semen, vaginal fluid, pre-ejaculate, or breast milk. Within these bodily fluids, HIV is present as both free virus particles and virus within infected immune cells. The four major routes of transmission are unprotected sexual intercourse, contaminated needles, breast milk, and transmission from an infected mother to her baby at birth.

TETANUS

Tetanus is a communicable disease that is characterized by a prolonged contraction of skeletal muscle fibres. The primary symptoms are caused by tetanospasmin, a neurotoxin produced by the Gram-positive, obligate anaerobic bacterium Clostridium tetani. Infection generally occurs through wound contamination, and often involves a cut or deep puncture wound. As the infection progresses, muscle spasms in the jaw develop, hence the common name, lockjaw. This is followed by difficulty in swallowing and general muscle stiffness and spasms in other parts of the body. Infection can be prevented by proper immunization and by post-exposure.

Prevention

Tetanus can be prevented by vaccination. The CDC recommends that adults receive a booster vaccine every ten years, and standard care practice in many places is to give the booster to any patient with a puncture wound who is uncertain of when he or she was last vaccinated, or if he or she has had fewer than 3 lifetime doses of the vaccine. The booster cannot prevent a potentially fatal case of tetanus from the current wound, however, as it can take up to two weeks for tetanus antibodies to form. In children under the age of seven, the tetanus vaccine is often administered as a combined vaccine, DPT vaccine, which also includes vaccines against diptheria and pertussis. For adults and children over seven, the TD vaccine (Tetanus and Diptheria) or TDAP (Tetanus, Diptheria, and Acellular Pertussis) is commonly used.

LEPROSY

Leprosy or *Hansen's disease,* is a chronic disease caused by the bacterium Mycobacterium leprae. Leprosy is primarily a granulomatous disease of the peripheral nerves and mucosa of the upper respiratory tract; skin lesions are the primary external symptoms. Left untreated, leprosy can be progressive, causing permanent damage to the skin, nerves, limbs and eyes. Contrary to popular belief, leprosy does not actually cause body parts to simply fall off.

Prevention

Single dose of rifampicin is able to reduce the rate of leprosy in contacts by 57% to 75%. BCG is able to offer a variable amount of protection against leprosy as well as against tuberculosis.

HEPATITIS

Hepatitis implies injury to the liver characterized by the presence of inflammatory cells in the tissue of the organ. The condition can be self-limiting, healing on its own, or can progress to scarring of the liver. Hepatitis is acute when it lasts less than six months and chronic when it persists longer. A group of viruses known as the *hepatitis viruses* cause most cases of liver damage worldwide. Hepatitis can also be due to toxins (notably alcohol), other infections or from autoimmune process. It may run a subclinical course when the affected person may not feel ill. The patient becomes unwell and symptomatic when the disease impairs liver functions that include, among other things, removal of harmful substances, regulation of blood composition, and production of bile to help digestion.

Signs and Symptoms

Acute hepatitis: Hepatitis A is an acute infectious disease of the liver caused by Hepatitis A virus, which is most commonly transmitted by the faecal-oral route via contaminated food or drinking water. Acute viral hepatitis is more likely to be asymptomatic in younger people. Symptomatic individuals may present after convalescent stage of 7 to 10 days, with the total illness lasting 2 to 6 weeks.

Initial features are of nonspecific flu-like symptoms, common to almost all acute viral infections and may include malaise, muscle and joint aches, fever, nausea or vomiting, diarrhoea, and headache. More specific symptoms, which can be present in acute hepatitis from any cause, are: profound loss of appetite, aversion to smoking among smokers, dark urine, yellowing of the eyes and skin (i.e., jaundice) and abdominal discomfort.

Chronic Hepatitis: Majority of patients will remain asymptomatic or mildly symptomatic, abnormal blood tests being the only manifestation. Features may be related to the extent of liver damage or the cause of hepatitis. Many experience return of symptoms related to acute hepatitis. Jaundice can be a late feature and may indicate extensive damage. Other features include abdominal fullness from enlarged liver or spleen, low grade fever and fluid retention (ascites). Extensive damage and scarring of liver (i.e., cirrhosis) leads to weight loss, easy bruising and bleeding tendencies. Acne, abnormal menstruation, lung scarring, inflammation of the thyroid gland and kidneys may be present in women with autoimmune hepatitis.

Hepatitis B virus infects the liver of hominoidae, including humans, and causes an inflammation called hepatitis. It is a DNA virus and one of many unrelated viruses that cause viral hepatitis. The acute illness causes liver inflammation, vomiting, jaundice and — rarely — death. ***Chronic hepatitis B*** may eventually cause liver cirrhosis and liver cancer — a fatal disease with very poor response to current chemotherapy. The infection is preventable by vaccination.

Hepatitis C is a *blood-borne infectious* disease that is caused by the hepatitis C virus (HCV), affecting the liver. The hepatitis C virus (HCV) is spread by blood-to-blood contact. The infection is often asymptomatic, but once established, ***chronic infection*** can cause inflammation of the liver (chronic hepatitis). This condition can progress to scarring of the liver (fibrosis), and advanced scarring (cirrhosis). In some cases, those with cirrhosis will go on to develop liver failure or other complications of cirrhosis, including liver cancer.

Hepatitis D is a disease caused by a small circular RNA virus (Hepatitis delta virus or hepatitis D virus, HDV). HDV is considered to be a subviral satellite because it can propagate only in the presence of another virus, the ***hepatitis B*** virus (HBV). Transmission of HDV can occur either via simultaneous infection with HBV (coinfection) or via infection of an individual previously infected with HBV (superinfection).

Hepatitis E is a *viral hepatitis* (liver inflammation) caused by infection with a virus called hepatitis E virus (HEV).

FOOD POISONING

Food-borne illness (also food-borne disease and colloquially referred to as food poisoning) is any illness resulting from the consumption of food.

There are two types of food poisoning—*food infection* and *food intoxication*. Food infection refers to the presence of bacteria or other microbes which infect the body after consumption. Food intoxication refers to the ingestion of toxins contained within the food, including bacterially produced exotoxins, which can happen even when the microbe that produced the toxin is no longer present or able to cause infection. In spite of the common term food poisoning, most cases are caused by a variety of pathogenic bacteria, viruses, prions or parasites that contaminate food, rather than chemical or natural toxins.

Causes

Food-borne illness usually arises from improper handling, preparation, or food storage. Good hygiene practices before, during, and after food preparation can reduce the chances of contracting an illness. The action of monitoring food to ensure that it will not cause food-borne illness is known as food safety. Food-borne disease can also be caused by a large variety of toxins that affect the environment.

Food-borne illness can also be caused by pesticides or medicines in food and naturally toxic substances like poisonous mushrooms or reef fish.

Symptoms and Mortality

Symptoms typically begin several hours to several days after consumption and depending on the agent involved, can include one or more of the following: nausea, abdominal pain, vomiting, diarrhoea, gastroenteritis, fever, headache or fatigue.

In most cases the body is able to permanently recover after a short period of acute discomfort and illness. However, food-borne illness can result in permanent health problems or even death, especially for people at high risk, including babies, young children, pregnant women (and their foetuses), elderly people, sick people and others with weak immune systems.

Food-borne illness is a major cause of reactive arthritis, which typically occurs 1–3 weeks afterward. Similarly, people with liver disease are especially susceptible to infections from Vibrio vulnificus, which can be found in oysters or crabs.

Tetrodotoxin poisoning from reef fish and other animals manifests rapidly as numbness and shortness of breath, and is often fatal.

STUDY QUESTIONS

Write short notes on the following:

(a) Communicable diseases;

(b) Threadworm infection; and

(c) Sexually-transmitted disease.

■■■

9

Non-Communicable Diseases

NON-COMMUNICABLE DISEASES

A non-communicable disease or NCD is a disease which is not infectious. Such diseases may result from genetic or lifestyle factors. A non-communicable disease is an illness that is caused by something other than a pathogen. It might result from hereditary factors, improper diet, smoking, or other factors. Those resulting from lifestyle factors are sometimes called diseases of affluence. Examples include hypertension, diabetes, cardiovascular disease, cancer, and mental health problems, asthma, etc. The non-communicable diseases are spread by: heredity, surroundings and behaviour.

HYPERTENSION

Hypertension, also referred to as high blood pressure, HTN or HPN, is a medical condition in which the blood pressure is chronically elevated. In current usage, the word "hypertension" without a qualifier normally refers to arterial hypertension.

Hypertension can be classified either essential (primary) or secondary. Essential hypertension indicates that no specific medical cause can be found to explain a patient's condition. Secondary hypertension indicates that the high blood pressure is a result of (i.e., secondary to) another condition, such as kidney disease or tumours (pheochromocytoma and paraganglioma). Persistent hypertension is one of the risk factors for strokes, heart attacks, heart failure and arterial aneurysm, and is a leading cause of chronic renal failure. Even moderate elevation of arterial blood pressure leads to shortened life expectancy. At severely high pressures, defined as mean arterial pressures 50% or more above average, a person can expect to live no more than a few years unless appropriately treated.

In individuals older than 50 years, hypertension is considered to be present when a person's systolic blood pressure is consistently 140 mm Hg or greater. Prehypertension is defined as blood pressure from 120/80 mm Hg to 139/89 mm Hg.

Causes

Although no specific medical cause can be determined in essential hypertension, it often has several contributing factors. These include *obesity, salt sensitivity, renin homeostasis, insulin resistance, genetics*, and age.

Diagnosis of hypertension is generally on the basis of a persistently high blood pressure. Usually this requires three separate measurements at least one week apart. Exceptionally, if the elevation is extreme, or end-organ damage is present then the diagnosis may be applied and treatment commenced immediately.

Obtaining reliable blood pressure measurement relies on following several rules and understanding the many factors that influence blood pressure reading.

For instance, measurements in control of hypertension should be at least 1 hour after caffeine, 30 minutes after smoking or strenuous exercise and without any stress. Cuff size is also important. The bladder should encircle and cover two-thirds of the length of the (upper) arm. The patient should be sitting upright in a chair with both feet flat on the floor for a minimum of five minutes prior to taking a reading. The patient should not be on any adrenergic stimulants, such as those found in many cold medications.

Prevention

Prevention of hypertension only goes as far as the cause; one can adjust lifestyle related causes but genetics, race, age and gender are outside the realm of change.

Modifiable factors include diet, weight-loss, exercise and stress management.

Low-sodium and low-fat diets can reduce cardiovascular risks and keep arteries clear of plaque and blood volume at normal levels.

Losing even 10% of body weight can have fantastic benefits towards health, including reversal or prevention of HTN, dropping systolic pressures several points.

Exercise maintains a healthy heart, thus healthy cardiac contractions and functions. The heart is a muscle too, working out the cardiac muscles makes the heart beat more efficiently, thus pumping blood around the body more effectively.

Stressors can negatively affect blood pressure by activating the sympathetic nervous system, thus fight or flight responses which increase heart-rate and blood pressure. Chronic stress can lead to regular and frequent activation of the system and repeated high blood pressure.

DIABETES

Diabetes is a syndrome of disordered metabolism, usually due to a combination of hereditary and environmental causes, resulting in abnormally high blood sugar levels (hyperglycemia). Blood glucose levels are controlled by a complex interaction of multiple chemicals and hormones in the body, including the hormone insulin made in the beta cells of the pancreas. Diabetes mellitus refers to the group of diseases that lead to high blood glucose levels due to defects in either insulin secretion or insulin action.

Diabetes develops due to a diminished production of insulin (in type 1) or resistance to its effects (in type 2 and gestational). Both lead to hyperglycaemia, which largely causes the acute signs of diabetes: excessive urine production, resulting compensatory thirst and increased fluid intake, blurred vision, unexplained weight loss, lethargy, and changes in energy metabolism.

The injections by a syringe, insulin pump, or insulin pen deliver insulin, which is a basic treatment of type 1 diabetes.

Diabetes and its *treatments* can cause many complications. Acute complications (hypoglycemia, ketoacidosis, or nonketotic hyperosmolar coma) may occur if the disease is not adequately controlled. Serious long-term complications include cardiovascular disease (doubled risk), chronic renal failure, retinal damage (which can lead to blindness), nerve damage (of several kinds), and microvascular damage, which may cause impotence and poor wound healing. Poor healing of wounds, particularly of the feet, can lead to gangrene, and possibly to amputation. Adequate treatment of diabetes, as well as increased emphasis on blood pressure control and lifestyle factors (such as not smoking and maintaining a healthy body weight), may improve the risk profile of most of the chronic complications. In the developed world, diabetes is the most significant cause of adult blindness in the non-elderly and the leading cause of non-traumatic amputation in adults, and diabetic nephropathy is the main illness requiring renal dialysis.

Signs and Symptoms

The classical triad of diabetes symptoms is polyuria, polydipsia and polyphagia, which are, respectively, frequent urination, increased thirst and consequent increased fluid intake, and increased appetite. Symptoms may develop quite rapidly (weeks or months) in type 1 diabetes, particularly in children. However, in type 2 diabetes symptoms usually develop much more slowly and may be subtle or completely absent. Type 1 diabetes may also cause a rapid yet significant weight loss (despite normal or even increased eating) and irreducible fatigue. All of these symptoms except weight loss can also manifest in type 2 diabetes in patients whose diabetes is poorly controlled.

When the glucose concentration in the blood is raised beyond its renal threshold, reabsorption of glucose in the proximal renal tubuli is incomplete, and part of the glucose remains in the urine (glycosuria). This increases the osmotic pressure of the urine and inhibits reabsorption of water by the kidney, resulting in increased urine production (polyuria) and increased fluid loss. Lost blood volume will be replaced osmotically from water held in body cells and other body compartments, causing dehydration and increased thirst.

CARDIOVASCULAR DISEASE

Cardiovascular disease or cardiovascular diseases refers to the class of diseases that involve the heart or blood vessels (arteries and veins). While the term technically refers to any disease that affects the cardiovascular system (as used in MeSH), it is usually used to refer to those related to atherosclerosis (arterial disease). These conditions have similar causes, mechanisms, and treatments. In practice, cardiovascular disease is treated by cardiologists, thoracic surgeons, vascular surgeons, neurologists, and interventional radiologists, depending on the organ system that is being treated. There is considerable overlap in the specialties, and it is common for certain procedures to be performed by different types of specialists in the same hospital.

By the time that heart problems are detected, the underlying cause (atherosclerosis) is usually quite advanced, having progressed for decades. There is therefore increased emphasis on preventing atherosclerosis by modifying risk factors, such as healthy eating, exercise and avoidance of smoking.

Types of Cardiovascular Diseases

- Aneurysm
- Angina
- Atherosclerosis
- Cerebrovascular Accident (Stroke)
- Cerebrovascular Disease
- Congestive Heart Failure
- Coronary Artery Disease
- Myocardial infarction (Heart Attack).

Prevention

Attempts to prevent cardiovascular disease are more effective when they remove and prevent causes, and they often take the form of modifying risk factors. Some factors, such as gender, age, and family history, cannot be modified. Smoking cessation (or abstinence) is one of the most effective and easily modifiable changes. Regular cardiovascular exercise (aerobic exercise) complements healthy eating habits. According to the American Heart Association, build-up of plaque on the arteries (atherosclerosis), partly as a result of high cholesterol and fat diet, is a leading cause for cardiovascular diseases. The combination of healthy diet and exercise is a means to improve serum cholesterol levels and reduce risks of cardiovascular diseases; if not, a physician may prescribe "cholesterol-lowering" drugs, such as the statins. These medications have additional protective benefits aside from their lipoprotein profile improvement. Aspirin may also be prescribed, as it has been shown to decrease the clot formation that may lead to myocardial infarctions and strokes; it is routinely prescribed for patients with one or more cardiovascular risk factors.

Cardiovascular Disease and Salt

There is evidence from one large unblinded randomised controlled trial of more than 3000 patients that reducing the amount of sodium in the diet reduced the risk of cardiovascular events by more than 25%.

Oral Hygiene and Cardiovascular Disease

Many recent clinical research discuss the direct relation between poor oral hygiene and cardiovascular disease. Oral bacteria and periodontal disease may trigger the inflammation in the coronary arteries and contribute to atherosclerosis (artery hardening and narrowing); same bacteria may determine the clot formation increasing the risk of heart attack or cerebral stroke.

Treatment

Treatment of cardiovascular disease depends on the specific form of the disease in each patient, but effective treatment always includes preventive lifestyle changes discussed above. Medications, such as blood pressure reducing medications, aspirin and the statin cholesterol-lowering drugs may be helpful. In some circumstances, surgery or angioplasty may be warranted to reopen, repair, or replace damaged blood vessels.

CANCER

Cancer (medical term: malignant neoplasm) is a class of diseases in which a group of cells display uncontrolled growth (division beyond the normal limits), invasion (intrusion on and destruction of adjacent tissues), and sometimes metastasis (spread to other locations in the body via lymph or blood). These three malignant properties of cancers differentiate them from benign tumors, which are self-limited, do not invade or metastasize. Most cancers form a tumour but some, like leukemia, do not. The branch of medicine concerned with the study, diagnosis, treatment, and prevention of cancer is oncology. Cancer may affect people at all ages, even foetuses, but the risk for most varieties increases with age. Cancer causes about 13% of all deaths.

Nearly all cancers are caused by abnormalities in the genetic material of the transformed cells. These abnormalities may be due to the effects of carcinogens, such as tobacco smoke, radiation, chemicals, or infectious agents. Other cancer-promoting genetic abnormalities may be randomly acquired through errors in DNA replication, or are inherited, and thus present in all cells from birth. The heritability of cancers is usually affected by complex interactions between carcinogens and the host's genome. New aspects of the genetics of cancer pathogenesis, such as DNA methylation, and microRNAs are increasingly recognized as important.

Genetic abnormalities found in cancer typically affect two general classes of genes. Cancer-promoting oncogenes are typically activated in cancer cells, giving those cells new properties, such as hyperactive growth and division, protection against programmed cell death, loss of respect for normal tissue boundaries, and the ability to become established in diverse tissue environments. Tumor suppressor genes are then inactivated in cancer cells, resulting in the loss of normal functions in those cells, such as accurate DNA replication, control over the cell cycle, orientation and adhesion within tissues, and interaction with protective cells of the immune system.

Diagnosis usually requires the histologic examination of a tissue biopsy specimen by a pathologist, although the initial indication of malignancy can be symptoms or radiographic imaging abnormalities. Most cancers can be treated and some cured, depending on the specific type, location, and stage. Once diagnosed, cancer is usually treated with a combination of surgery, chemotherapy and radiotherapy. As research develops, treatments are becoming more specific for different varieties of cancer. There has been significant progress in the development of targeted therapy drugs that act specifically on detectable molecular abnormalities in certain tumors, and which minimize damage to normal cells. The prognosis of cancer patients is most influenced by the type of cancer, as well as the stage, or extent of the disease. In addition, histologic grading and the presence of specific molecular markers can also be useful in establishing prognosis, as well as in determining individual treatments.

Signs and Symptoms

Roughly, cancer symptoms can be divided into three groups:

Local symptoms: unusual lumps or swelling (tumor), hemorrhage (bleeding), pain and/or ulceration. Compression of surrounding tissues may cause symptoms such as jaundice (yellowing the eyes and skin).

Symptoms of metastasis (spreading): enlarged lymph nodes, cough and hemoptysis, hepatomegaly (enlarged liver), bone pain, fracture of affected bones and neurological symptoms. Although advanced cancer may cause pain, it is often not the first symptom.

Systemic symptoms: weight loss, poor appetite, fatigue and cachexia (wasting), excessive sweating (night sweats), anemia and specific paraneoplastic phenomena, i.e., specific conditions that are due to an active cancer, such as thrombosis or hormonal changes.

Every symptom in the above list can be caused by a variety of conditions (a list of which is referred to as the differential diagnosis). Cancer may be a common or uncommon cause of each item.

Causes

Cancer is a diverse class of diseases which differ widely in their causes and biology. The common thread in all known cancers is the acquisition of abnormalities in the genetic material of the cancer cell and its progeny. Research into the pathogenesis of cancer can be divided into three broad areas of focus. The *first* area of research focuses on the agents and events which cause or facilitate genetic changes in cells destined to become cancer. *Second,* it is important to uncover the precise nature of the genetic damage, and the genes which are affected by it. The *third* focus is on the consequences of those genetic changes on the biology of the cell, both in generating the defining properties of a cancer cell, and in facilitating additional genetic events, leading to further progression of the cancer.

Prevention

Cancer prevention is defined as active measures to decrease the incidence of cancer. This can be accomplished by avoiding carcinogens or altering their metabolism, pursuing a lifestyle or diet that modifies cancer-causing factors and/or medical intervention (chemoprevention, treatment of pre-malignant lesions). The epidemiological concept of "prevention" is usually defined as either primary prevention, for people who have not been diagnosed with a particular disease, or secondary prevention, aimed at reducing recurrence or complications of a previously diagnosed illness.

Observational epidemiological studies that show associations between risk factors and specific cancers mostly serve to generate hypotheses about potential interventions that could reduce cancer incidence or morbidity. Randomized controlled trials then test whether hypotheses generated by epidemiological trials and laboratory research actually result in reduced cancer incidence and mortality. In many cases, findings from observational epidemiological studies are not confirmed by randomized controlled trials.

About a third of the twelve most common cancers worldwide are due to nine potentially modifiable risk factors. Men with cancer are twice as likely as women to have a modifiable risk factor for their disease. The nine risk factors are tobacco smoking, excessive alcohol use, diet low in fruit and vegetables, limited physical exercise, human papillomavirus infection (unsafe sex), urban air pollution, domestic use of solid fuels, and contaminated injections (hepatitis B and C).

MENTAL HEALTH

Mental health is a term used to describe either a level of cognitive or emotional wellbeing or an absence of a mental disorder. From perspectives of the discipline of positive psychology or holism mental health may include an individual's ability to enjoy life and procure a balance between life activities and efforts to achieve psychological resilience.

The World Health Organization defines mental health as "a state of well-being in which the individual realizes his or her own abilities, can cope with the normal stresses of life, can work productively and fruitfully, and is able to make a contribution to his or her community." It was previously stated that there was no one "official" definition of mental health. Cultural differences, subjective assessments, and competing professional theories all affect how "mental health" is defined.

Mental health can be seen as a continuum, where an individual's mental health may have many different possible values. Mental wellness is generally viewed as a positive attribute, such that a person can reach enhanced levels of mental health, even if they do not have any diagnosable mental health condition. This definition of mental health highlights emotional well-being, the capacity to live a full and creative life, and the flexibility to deal with life's inevitable challenges. Many therapeutic systems and self-help books offer methods and philosophies espousing strategies and techniques vaunted as effective for further improving the mental wellness of otherwise healthy people. Positive psychology is increasingly prominent in mental health.

A holistic model of mental health generally includes concepts based upon anthropological, educational, psychological, religious and sociological perspectives, as well as theoretical perspectives from personality, social, clinical, health and developmental psychology.

An example of a wellness model includes one developed by Myers, Sweeny and Witmer. It includes five life tasks — essence or spirituality, work and leisure, friendship, love and self-direction—and twelve sub tasks—sense of worth, sense of control, realistic beliefs, emotional awareness and coping, problem solving and creativity, sense of humour, nutrition, exercise, self-care, stress management, gender identity, and cultural identity—are identified as characteristics of healthy functioning and a major component of wellness. The components provide a means of responding to the circumstances of life in a manner that promotes healthy functioning.

BLINDNESS

Blindness is the condition of lacking visual perception due to physiological or neurological factors.

Various scales have been developed to describe the extent of vision loss and define "blindness." Total blindness is the complete lack of form and visual light perception and is clinically recorded as "NLP," an abbreviation for "no light perception." Blindness is frequently used to describe severe visual impairment with residual vision. Those described as having only "light perception" have no more sight than the ability to tell light from dark. A person with only "light projection" can tell the general direction of a light source.

In order to determine which people may need special assistance because of their visual disabilities, various governmental jurisdictions have formulated more complex definitions referred to as legal blindness. Legal blindness is defined as visual acuity (vision) of 20/200 (6/60) or less in the better eye with best correction possible. This means that a legally blind individual would have to stand 20 feet (6.1 m) from an object to see it—with vision correction—with the same degree of clarity as a normally sighted person could from 200 feet (61 m). In many areas, people with average acuity who nonetheless have a visual field of less than 20 degrees (the norm being 180 degrees) are also classified as being legally blind. Approximately ten percent of those deemed legally blind, by any measure, have no vision. The rest have some vision, from light perception alone to relatively good acuity. Low vision is sometimes used to describe visual acuities from 20/70 to 20/200.

CAUSES OF BLINDNESS

Serious visual impairment has a variety of causes:

Diseases

The most common causes of blindness around the world are:
cataracts (47.8%),
glaucoma (12.3%),
uveitis (10.2%),
age-related macular degeneration (AMD) (8.7%),
trachoma (3.6%),
corneal opacity (5.1%), and
diabetic retinopathy (4.8%), among other causes.

People in developing countries are significantly more likely to experience visual impairment as a consequence of treatable or preventable conditions than are their counterparts in the developed world. While vision impairment is most common in people over age 60 across all regions, children in poorer communities are more likely to be affected by blinding diseases than are their more affluent peers.

In developing countries, wherein people have shorter life expectancies, cataracts and water-borne parasites—both of which can be treated effectively—are most often the culprits (see River blindness, for example). Of the estimated 40 million blind people located around the world, 70–80% can have some or all of their sight restored through treatment.

In developed countries where parasitic diseases are less common and cataract surgery is more available, age-related macular degeneration, glaucoma, and diabetic retinopathy are usually the leading causes of blindness.

Abnormalities and Injuries

Eye injuries, most often occurring in people under 30, are the leading cause of monocular blindness (vision loss in one eye) throughout the United States. Injuries and cataracts affect the eye itself, while abnormalities such as optic nerve hypoplasia affect the nerve bundle that sends signals from the eye to the back of the brain, which can lead to decreased visual acuity. People with injuries to the occipital lobe of the brain can, despite having undamaged eyes and optic nerves, still be legally or totally blind.

Genetic Defects

People with albinism often suffer from visual impairment to the extent that many are legally blind, though few of them actually cannot see. Leber's congenital amaurosis can cause total blindness or severe sight loss from birth or early childhood. Recent advances in mapping of the human genome have identified other genetic causes of low vision or blindness. One such example is Bardet-Biedl syndrome.

Poisoning

Rarely, blindness is caused by the intake of certain chemicals. A well-known example is methanol, which ironically is only mildly toxic and minimally intoxicating, but when not competing with ethanol for metabolism, methanol breaks down into the substances formaldehyde and formic acid which in turn can cause blindness, an array of other health complications, and death. Methanol is commonly found in methylated spirits, denatured ethyl alcohol, to avoid paying taxes on selling ethanol intended for human consumption. Methylated spirits are sometimes used by alcoholics as a desperate and cheap substitute for regular ethanol alcoholic beverages.

STROKE

A stroke is the rapidly developing loss of brain functions due to a disturbance in the blood vessels supplying blood to the brain.

This can be due to ischemia (lack of blood supply) caused by thrombosis or embolism or due to a hemorrhage. As a result, the affected area of the brain is unable to function, leading to inability to move one or more limbs on one side of the body, inability to understand or formulate speech or inability to see one side of the visual field. In the past, stroke was referred to as cerebrovascular accident or CVA, but the term "stroke" is now preferred.

A stroke is a medical emergency and can cause permanent neurological damage, complications and death. It is the number two cause of death worldwide and may soon become the leading cause of death worldwide. Risk factors for stroke include advanced age, hypertension (high blood pressure), previous stroke or transient ischemic attack (TIA), diabetes, high cholesterol, cigarette smoking and atrial fibrillation. High blood pressure is the most important modifiable risk factor of stroke.

Stroke is occasionally treated with thrombolysis ("clot buster"), but usually with supportive care (speech and language therapy, physiotherapy and occupational therapy) in a "stroke unit" and secondary prevention with antiplatelet drugs (aspirin and often dipyridamole), blood pressure control, statins, and in selected patients with carotid endarterectomy and anticoagulation.

Signs and Symptoms

Stroke symptoms typically start suddenly, over seconds to minutes, and in most cases don't progress further. The symptoms depend on the area of the brain affected. The more extensive the area of brain affected, the more functions that are likely to be lost. Some forms of stroke can cause additional symptoms: in intracranial hemorrhage, the affected area may compress other structures. Most forms of stroke are not associated with headache, apart from subarachnoid hemorrhage and cerebral venous thrombosis and occasionally intracerebral hemorrhage.

Prevention

Given the disease burden of stroke, prevention is an important public health concern. Primary prevention is less effective than secondary prevention (as judged by the number needed to treat to prevent one stroke per year). Because stroke may indicate underlying atherosclerosis, it is important to determine the patient's risk for other cardiovascular diseases such as coronary heart disease. Conversely, aspirin prevents against first stroke in patients who have suffered a myocardial infarction.

Risk Factors

The most important modifiable risk factors for stroke are high blood pressure and atrial fibrillation. Other modifiable risk factors include high blood cholesterol levels, diabetes, cigarette smoking (active and passive), heavy alcohol consumption and drug use, lack of physical activity, obesity and unhealthy diet. Alcohol use could predispose to ischemic stroke, and intracerebral and subarachnoid hemorrhage via multiple mechanisms (for example, hypertension, atrial fibrillation, rebound thrombocytosis and platelet aggregation and clotting disturbances). The drugs most commonly associated with stroke are cocaine, amphetamines causing hemorrhagic stroke, but also over-the-counter cough and cold drugs containing sympathomimetics.

No high quality studies have shown the effectiveness of interventions aimed at weight reduction, promotion of regular exercise, reducing alcohol consumption or smoking cessation. Nonetheless, given the large body of circumstantial evidence, best medical management for stroke includes advice on diet, exercise, smoking and alcohol use. Medication or drug therapy is the most common method of stroke prevention; carotid endarterectomy can be a useful surgical method of preventing stroke.

Treatment

Ideally, people who have had a stroke are admitted to a "stroke unit", a ward or dedicated area in hospital staffed by nurses and therapists with experience in stroke. It has been shown that people admitted to a stroke unit have a higher chance of surviving than those admitted elsewhere in hospital, even if they are being cared for by doctors with experience in stroke.

When an acute stroke is suspected by history and physical examination, the goal of early assessment is to determine the cause.

Treatment varies according to the underlying cause of the stroke, thromboembolic (ischemic) or hemorrhagic. A non-contrast head CT scan can rapidly identify a hemorrhagic stroke by imaging bleeding in or around the brain. If no bleeding is seen, a presumptive diagnosis of ischemic stroke is made.

STUDY QUESTIONS

1. What do you understand by Non-Communicable Disease ?
2. Write short notes on the following:
   (a) Hypertension;
   (b) Diabetes;
   (c) Cardiovascular Disease;
   (d) Cancer;
   (e) Mental health; and
   (f) Blindness.

■■■

10

Epidemiology

INTRODUCTION

Epidemiology is the study of factors affecting the health and illness of populations, and serves as the foundation and logic of interventions made in the interest of public health and preventive medicine. It is considered a cornerstone methodology of public health research, and is highly regarded in evidence-based medicine for identifying risk factors for disease and determining optimal treatment approaches to clinical practice. In the work of communicable and non-communicable diseases, the work of epidemiologists ranges from outbreak investigation to study design, data collection and analysis, including the development of statistical models to test hypotheses and the documentation of results for submission to peer-reviewed journals. Epidemiologists may draw on a number of other scientific disciplines such as biology in understanding disease processes and social science disciplines, including sociology and philosophy in order to better understand proximate and distal risk factors.

EPIDEMIC

In epidemiology, an infection that is *epidemic* appears as new cases in a given human population, during a given period, at a rate that substantially exceeds what is "expected," based on recent experience (the number of new cases in the population during a specified period of time is called the "incidence rate"). (An epizootic is the analogous circumstance within an animal population.) In recent usages, the disease is not required to be communicable.The term "epidemic" is often used in a sense to refer to widespread and growing societal problems, for example, in discussions of obesity, mental illness or drug addiction.

USES OF EPIDEMIOLOGY

Public health needs more epidemiology—this is the most obvious intellectual basis for its further advance. Epidemiology, moreover, as a tried instrument of research—with its modern developments in sampling and surveys, small-number statistics, the follow-up of cohorts, international comparisons, field experiment and family study; and with its extensions to problems of genetics as well as environment, to physiological norms as well as disease, the psychological as well as the physical, morbidity as well as mortality—epidemiology now offers the possibility of a new era of collaboration between public health workers and clinical medicine. Such a collaboration could be on equal terms, each making their particular contribution to the joint solving of problems. There is abundant evidence today that clinicians would very much welcome such a development.

Medicine as a whole needs more epidemiology, for without it cardinal areas have to be excluded from the consideration of human health and sickness. Epidemiology, moreover, is rich with suggestions for clinical and laboratory study, and it offers many possibilities for testing hypotheses emerging from these. One of the most urgent social needs of the day is to identify rules of healthy living that might do for us what Snow and others did for the Victorians, and help to reduce the burden of illness in middle and old age which is so characteristic a feature of our society. There is no indication whatever that the experimental sciences alone will be able to produce the necessary guidance. Collaboration between clinician, laboratory scientist and epidemiologist might be more successful. The possibilities are at present unlimited, if often neglected.

MODES OF TRANSMISSION

In medicine, transmission is the passing of a disease from an infected individual or group to a previously uninfected individual or group. The micro-organisms (bacteria and viruses) that cause disease may be transmitted from one person to another by one or more of the following means:

- *Droplet contact* — coughing or sneezing on another person
- *Direct physical contact* — touching an infected person, including sexual contact
- *Indirect contact* — usually by touching soil contamination or a contaminated surface
- *Air-borne transmission* — if the micro-organism can remain in the air for long periods
- *Faecal-oral transmission* — usually from contaminated food or water sources
- *Vector-borne transmission* — carried by insects or other animals

Micro-organisms vary widely in the length of time that they can survive outside the human body, and so vary in how they are transmitted. Exposure occurs through either direct or indirect contact.

Direct transmission occurs when a pathogen, an agent that causes disease, esp. a living micro-organism such as a bacterium or fungus. is transmitted directly from an infected individual to you. For example, you could become infected with HBV Hepatitis B Virus if you had an open wound that came into contact with a patient's HBV infected blood.

Indirect transmission occurs when an inanimate object serves as a temporary reservoir for the infectious agent. For example, you could become infected with HBV if you come into contact with equipment that has dried infectious blood on it.

It is important to note that many diseases do not manifest themselves immediately. Therefore, it can often be difficult to track the source of an exposure.

Many of the symptoms of some diseases can be quite similar to the flu. Therefore, if flu-like symptoms do not subside in a normal amount of time with normal treatment methods, you may need to have blood tests performed to rule out other possible causes.

Pathogens can enter the body through four primary routes:

- Inhalation
- Contact with blood or other body fluids
- Ingestion
- Faecal-oral
- An intermediate carrier (such as a tick).

Air-borne diseases are spread when droplets of pathogens are expelled into the air due to coughing, sneezing or talking. Air-borne diseases of concern to emergency responders include:

- Meningitis Inflammation of the meninges of the brain and the spinal cord.
- Chickenpox
- Tuberculosis (TB)
- Influenza.

Many of these diseases require prolonged exposure for infection to occur, posing only minimal threat to emergency responders. However, there are preventive measures, such as wearing masks or maximizing ventilation, that help reduce these risks.

Blood-borne disease. As a first responder, you run the risk of encountering blood-borne pathogens. Exposure to blood-borne pathogens can occur through many mechanisms: needle sticks, being splashed with blood or body fluids on the mucous membranes (the mouth, eyes, and nose), even in some cases human bites (although the risk of transmission via human bites is extremely low). However, contact with blood-borne pathogens falls into two main categories:

Direct – via an open lesion on the skin or mucous membrane

Indirect – via punctures by contaminated sharps or needles.

Common blood-borne diseases of which first responders need to be aware include:

- Hepatitis B
- Hepatitis C
- Hepatitis D
- AIDS (Acquired Immunodeficiency Syndrome).

HIV/AIDS

Acquired Immunodeficiency Syndrome (AIDS) is a severe disease that represents the late stage of infection with the Human Immunodeficiency Virus (HIV), which causes defective functioning of the body's immune system.

AIDS was first recognized in the U.S. in the early 1980s, when two unusual diseases (Karposi's sarcoma, a type of cancer, and Pneumocystis carinii, an organism that causes pneumonia in people with impaired immune systems) began to appear in homosexual men. Since that time, our understanding of the disease has progressed rapidly, although measures to prevent the spread of the disease have lagged behind. It is not an understatement to say that AIDS is the most serious public health threat the world has seen in the past 50 years. There is no part of the U.S., or the world, for that matter, that can be considered "safe" from the threat of HIV and AIDS.

HIV is a virus of the type known as retroviruses. These viruses infect certain cells in the body, incorporating their viral genetic material into the cell's own DNA. The body's cells then begin to produce the virus, and in the process, may themselves be killed. In the case of HIV, this virus infects only selected cells in the body, of which the most important are certain infection-fighting white blood cells known as lymphocytes, specifically those lymphocytes known as *helper cells* (which can be identified because they carry a marker called "CD4"). HIV can also infect certain cells in the nervous system.

IMMUNITY

An antigen is an agent or substance which can be recognised by the body as 'foreign'. Often it is only one relatively small chemical group of a larger foreign, substance which acts as the antigen, for example a component of the cell wall of a bacterium. Most antigens are proteins, though carbohydrates may act as weak antigens.

The body reacts to antigens by making antibodies, themselves proteins, or special lymphocytes carrying an antibody-like component on their cell surface. These antibodies or lymphocyte components interact chemically with the antigen in a highly specific manner a bit like two pieces of a jigsaw. However, occasionally antibodies or lymphocyte components may 'fit' other similar antigens, in much the same way as a piece of a jigsaw will sometimes work with other bits it wasn't originally intended to.

When the antigen and antibody interact, they bind together to form an antigen/antibody complex, or immune complex, and this binding neutralises or brings about the destruction of the antigen.

Immunity due to antibody-like components of lymphocytes is referred to as cell-mediated immunity since the lymphocyte cells themselves interact with the antigen. Immunity conveyed by antibodies is referred to as humoral immunity since in most cases the antibodies reach their destination via the blood plasma.

TYPES OF IMMUNITY

These *innate* and *adaptive* defence mechanisms require mutual co-operation in order to be effective in fighting infection.

Innate immunity Innate immunity refers to non-specific defense mechanisms that come into play immediately or within hours of an antigen's appearance in the body. These mechanisms include physical barriers such as skin, chemicals in the blood, and immune system cells that attack foreign cells in the body. The innate immune response is activated by chemical properties of the antigen.

Adaptive immunity Adaptive immunity refers to antigen-specific immune response. The adaptive immune response is more complex than the innate. The antigen first must be processed and recognized. Once an antigen has been recognized, the adaptive immune system creates an army of immune cells specifically designed to attack that antigen. Adaptive immunity also includes a "memory" that makes future responses against a specific antigen more efficient.

IMMUNE SYSTEM

The human body has a tremendous capability for defence against invasion by foreign agents which includes disease producing micro-organisms known as *pathogens*.

The *immune system* is divided into ***non-specific*** mechanisms, which are aimed at foreign agents in general, and involve the phagocytic activity of certain leukocytes. ***Specific*** defence mechanisms aimed at particular pathogens or toxic agents.

The immune system is primarily a defensive system which protects the individual against a variety of foreign substances including micro-organisms, transplanted cells and irritants. The mechanisms involved are relevant to a wide variety of clinical situations, including immunity against infectious disease, the rejection of transplanted organs, compatibility of blood for transfusion, allergic disorders, autoimmune diseases and malignant conditions.

Although the agents conferring immunity, which are antibodies (specialised blood proteins) and components of certain lymphocytes, have been recognised since the end of the nineteenth century, immunity remains a subject of intensive research, and many questions remain unanswered.

There are also mechanisms which protect against specific noxious substances and agents. These mechanisms work most efficiently when the body has previously come into contact with the foreign substance. It is said that the mechanisms are acquired following exposure, and that the substance is in some way remembered. This is known as the ***specific or acquired immune system***. This specific immune system is subdivided into *cellular* and *humoral* components.

MECHANISMS FOR KILLING BACTERIA

There are many ways in which these cells are able to kill bacteria and other foreign bodies but basically they belong to two categories.

(I) OXYGEN-DEPENDENT MECHANISMS

Oxygen-dependent mechanisms basically result from the respiratory burst associated with the act of phagocytosis. This results in the release of two chemicals H_2O_2 (hydrogen peroxide) and HOCl (hydrochlorous acid). These are two very powerful chemicals that are able to break down the protective wall of bacteria and other micro-organisms.

Of clinical importance in "chronic granulomatous disease of childhood" a condition in which the enzymes required to produce these enzymes are missing. As a result neutrophils can ingest bacteria but cannot break them down.

(II) OXYGEN-INDEPENDENT MECHANISMS

Lysozyme: An enzyme that attacks cell wall of some bacteria (especially Gram+ve). Negative bacteria is lacking in people with Down's Syndrome and hence accounts for their susceptibility to certain infections.

Lactoferrin: A chemical which binds onto iron thus inhibiting cell growth especially in bacteria.

Major Basic Protein (MBP): A cationic protein is found in eosinophils principally active against parasitic infections such as roundworms, liver flukes etc.

Bactericidal Permeability Increasing Protein: As its name suggests this substance increases permeability of cell membrane of many micro-organisms making them more vulnerable to attack from other agents of the immune system.

In addition to this white blood cells produce a lower pH (more acidic) environment which adds to the anti-bacterial properties. Unfortunately these mechanisms are not 100% successful.

Most noticeably the Mycobacterium species that cause leprosy and tuberculosis can actually live inside phagocytic cells such as neutrophils and are thus protected against drugs and the specific defence mechanisms.

INFECTION

Infection is the growth of a parasitic organism within the body. (A parasitic organism is one that lives on or in another organism and draws its nourishment therefrom.) A person with an infection has another organism (a "germ") growing within him, drawing its nourishment from the person.

The term "infection" has some exceptions. For example, the normal growth of the usual bacterial flora in the intestinal tract is not usually considered an infection. The same consideration applies to the bacteria that normally inhabit the mouth. In an infection, the infecting organism seeks to utilize the host's resources to multiply (usually at the expense of the host). The infecting organism, or pathogen, interferes with the normal functioning of the host and can lead to chronic wounds, gangrene, loss of an infected limb, and even death. The host's response to infection is inflammation. Colloquially, a pathogen is usually considered a microscopic organism though the definition is broader, including faeces, parasites, fungi, viruses, prions, and viroids. A symbiosis between parasite and host, whereby the relationship is beneficial for the former but detrimental to the latter, is characterised as parasitism. The branch of medicine that focuses on infections and pathogens is infectious disease.

A secondary infection is an infection that occurs during or following treatment of another already existing primary infection.

BACTERIAL OR VIRAL INFECTION

Bacterial and viral infections can both cause similar symptoms such as malaise, fever, and chills. It can be difficult, even for a doctor to distinquish which is the cause of a specific infection. It is important to distinguish, because viral infections cannot be cured by antibiotics.

SOURCES OF INFECTION

Pathways of infection are ways in which pathogens may enter the body. The following are the most common:

- *Droplet Infection Pathway*: This is most common route of infection. This type of infection is contracted when infectious droplets are coughed or sneezed into the air and subsequently inhaled by another individual. Ex: TB.

- *Faecal/Oral Infection Pathway*: This is second most common route of infection, is usually a result of consuming contaminated water. Ex: Cholera.
- *Contact Infection Pathway*: This is a result of direct or indirect contact with the infectious host; often contracted through the skin. Ex: Athletes foot.
- *Sexual Infectious Pathway:* This is a result of Anal, Vaginal or Oral contact. Ex Genital Herpes.
- *Oral Infectious Pathway*: This is a minor infectious pathway that is transmitted through oral/oral contact.
- *Contaminated Blood*: Harmful microbes can enter your body through your bloodstream.
- *Infected food or water*: Dangerous microbes can enter through your mouth if you drink untreated water or swallow food that's uncooked or unwashed.
- *Disease-carrying creatures:* Harmful microbes can enter your body through close contact with infected creatures.
- *Germy air:* Dangerous microbes can spread through the air and enter your nose and mouth when you breathe.

GROWTH OF MICROBES

Bacterial growth is the division of one bacterium into two identical daughter cells during a process called binary fission. Hence, local doubling of the bacterial population occurs. Both daughter cells from the division do not necessarily survive. However, if the number surviving exceeds unity on average, the bacterial population undergoes exponential growth. The measurement of an exponential bacterial growth curve in batch culture was traditionally a part of the training of all microbiologists; the basic means requires bacterial enumeration (cell counting) by direct and individual (microscopic, flow cytometry, direct and bulk (biomass), indirect and individual (colony counting), or indirect and bulk (most probable number, turbidity, nutrient uptake) methods. Models reconcile theory with the measurements.

In autecological studies, bacterial growth in batch culture can be modelled with four different phases: lag phase, exponential or log phase, stationary phase, and death phase.

During *lag phase*, bacteria adapt themselves to growth conditions. It is the period where the individual bacteria are maturing and not yet able to divide. During the lag phase of the bacterial growth cycle, synthesis of RNA, enzymes and other molecules occurs.

During the *exponential phase* (sometimes called the *log phase*), the number of new bacteria appearing per unit time is proportional to the present population. This gives rise to the classic exponential growth curve, in which the logarithm of the population density rises linearly with time. The actual rate of this growth depends upon the growth conditions, which affect the frequency of cell division events and the probability of both daughter cells surviving. Exponential growth cannot continue indefinitely, however, because the medium is soon depleted of nutrients and enriched with wastes.

During *stationary phase*, the growth rate slows as a result of nutrient depletion and accumulation of toxic products. This phase is reached as the bacteria begin to exhaust the resources that are available to them.

At *death phase*, bacteria run out of nutrients and die. This basic batch culture growth model draws out and emphasizes aspects of bacterial growth which may differ from the growth of macrofauna. It emphasizes clonality, asexual binary division, the short development time relative to replication itself, the seemingly low death rate, the need to move from a dormant state to a reproductive state or to condition the media, and finally, the tendency of lab adapted strains to exhaust their nutrients.

In reality, even in batch culture, the four phases are not well defined. The cells do not reproduce in synchrony without explicit and continual prompting (as in experiments with stalked bacteria) and their logarithmic phase growth is often not ever a constant rate, but instead a slowly decaying rate, a constant stochastic response to pressures both to reproduce and to go dormant in the face of declining nutrient concentrations and increasing waste concentrations.

Batch culture is the most common laboratory growth environment in which bacterial growth is studied, but it is only one of many. It is ideally spatially unstructured and temporally structured. The bacterial culture is incubated in a closed vessel with a single batch of medium. In some experimental regimes, some of the bacterial culture is periodically removed to a fresh sterile media is added. In the extreme case, this leads to the continual renewal of the nutrients. This is a chemostat also known as continuous culture. It is ideally spatially unstructured and temporally unstructured, in an equilibrium state defined by the nutrient supply rate and the reaction of the bacteria. In comparison to batch culture, bacteria are maintained in exponential growth phase and the grow growth rate of the bacteria is known. Related devices include turbidostats and auxostats.

Bacterial growth can be suppressed with bacteriostats, without necessarily killing the bacteria. In a synecological, a true-to-nature situation, where more than one bacterial species is present, the growth of microbes is more dynamic and continual.

Liquid is not the only laboratory environment for bacterial growth. Spatially structured environments such as biofilms or agar surfaces present additional complex growth models.

TRANSMISSION OF INFECTION

An infectious disease is transmitted from some source. Defining the means of transmission plays an important part in understanding the biology of an infectious agent, and in addressing the disease it causes. Transmission may occur through several different mechanisms. *Respiratory diseases* and meningitis are commonly acquired by contact with aerosolized droplets, spread by sneezing, coughing, talking, kissing or even singing. *Gastrointestinal* diseases are often acquired by ingesting contaminated food and water. *Sexually transmitted diseases* are acquired through contact with bodily fluids, generally as a result of sexual activity. Some infectious agents may be spread as a result of contact with a contaminated, inanimate object (known as a fomite), such as a coin passed from one person to another, while other diseases penetrate the skin directly.

Transmission of infectious diseases may also involve a "vector". Vectors may be *mechanical* or *biological*. A mechanical vector picks up an infectious agent on the outside of its body and transmits it in a passive manner. An example of a mechanical vector is a housefly, which lands on cow dung, contaminating its appendages with bacteria from the faeces, and then lands on food prior to consumption. The pathogen never enters the body of the fly.

Culex mosquitos Culex quinque-fasciatus as shown are biological vectors that transmit West Nile Virus.In contrast, biological vectors harbor pathogens within their bodies and deliver pathogens to new hosts in an active manner, usually a bite. Biological vectors are often responsible for serious blood-borne diseases, such as malaria, viral encephalitis, Chagas disease, Lyme disease and African sleeping sickness. Biological vectors are usually, though not exclusively, arthropods, such as mosquitoes, ticks, fleas and lice. Vectors are often required in the life cycle of a pathogen. A common strategy, used to control vector-borne infectious diseases, is to interrupt the life-cycle of a pathogen, by killing the vector.

The relationship between virulence and transmission is complex, and has important consequences for the long-term evolution of a pathogen. Since it takes many generations for a microbe and a new host species to co-evolve, an emerging pathogen may hit its earliest victims especially hard. It is usually in the first wave of a new disease that death rates are highest. If a disease is rapidly fatal, the host may die before the microbe can get passed along to another host. However, this cost may be overwhelmed by the short-term benefit of higher infectiousness if transmission is linked to virulence, as it is, for instance, in the case of cholera (the explosive diarrhea aids the bacterium in finding new hosts) or many respiratory infections (sneezing and coughing create infectious aerosols).

SOME DEFINITION OF TRANSMISSION OF INFECTION

The ***Reservoir of Infection*** is the principal habitat from which an infectious agent may spread to cause disease. Examples may include human beings, the reservoir of infection for Corynebacterium diphtheriae; animals, the reservoir for salmonella infections; soil, the reservoir for Clostridium tetani or water, the reservoir for Legionella pneumophila.

The ***Source of Infection*** is the location from which an infection is acquired. This may be endogenous if the infection is acquired from the patient's own commensal flora or exogenous when the infection is acquired from a source external to the patient.

Most cases of *cystitis* are endogenous, being caused by coliforms from the patient's own gut. Food poisoning, on the other hand, is exogenous. Inanimate sources of infection are termed vehicles of infection and are sometimes also referred to as fomites.

The ***Mode of Transmission*** of an infection is the mechanism by which an infectious agent passes from its source to the person to be infected.

Cases of infection may be sporadic when they are not related to other cases or clustered in outbreaks. If an infection is continually present within a community, it is said to be endemic.

Epidemics occur when the number of cases of infection in a community rises significantly above the endemic level. What passes for 'significant' can be highly variable. A world-wide epidemic is known as pandemic.

Infections from one person to another, unrelated person are said to spread horizontally through the community. When mothers are the cause of congenital infections in their offspring, this is said to be vertical transmission.

MODES OF TRANSMITTING INFECTION

There are a number of modes of transmitting infections. They include: person-to-person spread, food-borne infection, water-borne infection, air-borne infection and insect-borne infection.

- *Person-to-person spread*. Spread of such infections may involve intermediate vectors.
- *Food-borne infection*: Food poisoning caused by Bacillus cereus, for example. Bacterial spores contaminate rice and survive boiling. If the rice is cooled and reheated, the spores may

germinate and the bacteria produce a heat-stable toxin that induces vomiting.

- *Water-borne infection*: Contaminated water can be the vector for diseases such as typhoid, cholera, dysentery, hepatitis A and poliomyelitis.
- *Air-borne infection*: Legionella pneumophila causes Legionnaire's disease. It can be found in many natural water sources but is commonly associated with poorly maintained air conditioning systems or rarely cleaned shower heads. Air-borne droplets from such sources act as the vector for Legionnaire's disease.
- *Insect-borne infection*: Many diseases are insect-borne. Historically the most important is the plague, caused by Yersinia pestis and transmitted by rat fleas.

DISINFECTION

Disinfectants are antimicrobial agents that are applied to non-living objects to destroy micro-organisms, the process of which is known as *disinfection*. Disinfectants should generally be distinguished from antibiotics that destroy micro-organisms within the body, and from antiseptics, which destroy microorganisms on living tissue. Sanitizers are substances that reduce the number of micro-organisms to a safe level. One official and legal version states that a sanitizer must be capable of killing 99.999%, known as a 5 log reduction, of a specific bacterial test population, and to do so within 30 seconds. The main difference between a sanitizer and a disinfectant is that at a specified use dilution, the disinfectant must have a higher kill capability for pathogenic bacteria compared to that of a sanitizer. Very few disinfectants and sanitizers can sterilise (the complete elimination of all micro-organisms), and those that can depend entirely on their mode of application. Bacterial endospores are most resistant to disinfectants, however some viruses and bacteria also possess some tolerance.

RELATIVE EFFECTIVENESS OF DISINFECTANTS

One way to compare disinfectants is to compare how well they do against a known disinfectant and rate them accordingly. Phenol is the standard, and the corresponding rating system is called the

"Phenol coefficient". The disinfectant to be tested is compared with phenol on a standard microbe (usually Salmonella typhi or Staphylococcus aureus). Disinfectants that are more effective than phenol have a coefficient > 1. Those that are less effective have a coefficient < 1.

HOME DISINFECTANTS

By far the most cost-effective home disinfectant is the commonly used *chlorine bleach* (a 5% solution of Sodium hypochlorite) which is effective against most common pathogens, including such difficult organisms as tuberculosis (mycobacterium tuberculosis), hepatitis B and C, fungi, and antibiotic-resistant strains of staphylococcus and enterococcus. It even has some disinfectant action against parasitic organisms. Positives are that it kills the widest range of pathogens of any inexpensive disinfectant; it is extremely powerful against viruses and bacteria at room temperature; it is commonly available and inexpensive; and it breaks down quickly into harmless components (primarily table salt and oxygen). Negatives are that it is caustic to the skin and eyes, especially at higher concentrations; like many common disinfectants, it degrades in the presence of organic substances; it has a strong odor; it is not effective against giardia lamblia and cryptosporidium; and extreme caution must be taken not to combine it with ammonia or any acid (such as vinegar as this may cause noxious gases to be formed). The best practice is not to add anything to household bleach except water. Dilute bleach can be tolerated on the skin for a period of time by most persons, as witnessed by the long exposure to extremely dilute "chlorine" (actually sodium or calcium hypochlorite) many children get in swimming pools.

To use chlorine bleach effectively, the surface or item to be disinfected must be clean. In the bathroom or when cleaning after pets, special caution must be taken to wipe up urine first, before applying chlorine, to avoid toxic gas by-products. A 1 to 20 solution in water is effective simply by being wiped on and left to dry. The user should wear rubber gloves and, in tight airless spaces, goggles. If parasitic organisms are suspected, it should be applied at 1 to 1 concentration, or even undiluted; extreme caution must be taken to avoid contact with eyes and mucous membranes. Protective goggles and good ventilation are mandatory when applying concentrated bleach.

Commercial bleach tends to lose strength over time, whenever the container is opened. Old containers of partially used bleach may no longer have the labelled concentration.

Where one does not want to risk the corrosive effects of bleach, alcohol-based disinfectants are reasonably inexpensive and quite safe. The great drawback to them is their rapid evaporation; sometimes effective disinfection can be obtained only by immersing an object in the alcohol.

The use of some antimicrobials such as triclosan, particularly in the uncontrolled home environment, is controversial because it may lead to the germs becoming resistant. Chlorine bleach and alcohol do not cause resistance because they are so completely lethal, in a very direct physical way.

PHYSICAL DISINFECTION

Cleaning is usually restricted in meaning to the physical removal of surface contaminants, usually with detergents or soap and water, ultrasound or other methods. While cleaning does remove soils and bacteria, cleaning does not include any component of virus or bacteria killing or inactivation though it does have the effect of *disinfection by mechanical* means (physical removal). Even the most thorough cleaning leaves micro-organisms on the surface of the item. The use of an ultrasonic cleaner with detergents is able to dislodge fine particles from surfaces that may be inaccessible by physical scrubbing or brushing. It is more diffiult but not impossible to sterilize a surface that has not been properly cleaned first.

Disinfection is the killing or inactivation of some of the micro-organisms on the surface of an object without the claim for killing or inactivating all micro-organisms. For tools and small objects this generally refers to the effect of immersion in a liquid "germicidal".

For items that can't be immersed in a liquid germicidal, the area or object must first be washed and then the surface coated, usually by spraying, and then allowed to air dry.

A liquid germicidal's effectiveness is dependent on contact of the germicidal liquid to the virus or bacteria to be killed but other factors such as pH, temperature and microbial load (concentration) also play a part which can defeat an intended level of disinfection.

Effective cleaning is the most important step because bacteria and viruses may survive beneath a layer of dirt, beneath grease, dried blood, or in crevices or places that are difficult to reach by cleaning that shield the organism from direct contact with the disinfectant. Disinfecting solutions require the object be effectively precleaned before liquid disinfection.

Needle bars and tubes for tattoo are sometimes allowed to be re-used if permitted by law, but they may not be used on more than one client without cleaning and sterilization (as contrasted to disinfected) between uses. Needles used in piercing may never be reused.

Liquid disinfectants require specific solution strengths and contact time so it is mandatory to be familiar with the product by reading and following the label instructions and warnings.

All disinfectants do not destroy all types of micro-organisms and some may leave harmful chemical residues which must be removed prior to sterilization or use. They are almost all harmful to humans and animals.While disinfectants used as soaking agents seem to add a margin of safety to the cleaning process, the use of disinfectants themselves present other dangers.

Application of alcohol, clorox or boiling is considered disinfection, not sterilization. Most HDs require biological testing to verify the process. These methods cannot be routinely tested for effectiveness.

Disinfectants (meaning hard surface disinfectants) within the tattoo and piercing environment are most appropriately used on potentially contaminated objects which do not require sterilization, such as certain tools, counters, lights, chairs, etc.. Disinfection by physical means, such as in an autoclave, is also effective when used at less than sterilizing requirements. In the US, disinfectants designed for use on the skin are usually called *antiseptics* to distinguish them as a separate group with different specifications.

ANTISEPTICS

Antiseptics are antimicrobial substances that are applied to living tissue/skin to reduce the possibility of infection, sepsis, or putrefaction. They should generally be distinguished from antibiotics that destroy bacteria within the body, and from disinfectants, which destroy micro-organisms found on non-living objects. Some antiseptics are true germicides, capable of destroying microbes (bacteriocidal), whilst others are bacteriostatic and only prevent or inhibit their growth. Antibacterials are antiseptics that only act against bacteria.

For the growth of bacteria there must be a certain food supply, moisture, in most cases oxygen, and a certain minimum temperature. These conditions have been specially studied and applied in connection with the preserving of food and in the ancient practice of embalming the dead, which is the earliest illustration of the systematic use of antiseptics.

In early inquiries a great point was made of the prevention of putrefaction, and work was done in the way of finding how much of an agent must be added to a given solution, in order that the bacteria accidentally present might not develop. But for various reasons this was an inexact method, and today an antiseptic is judged by its effects on pure cultures of definite pathogenic celicular single helix microbes, and on their vegetative and spore forms. Their standardization has been affected in many instances, and a water solution of phenol of a certain fixed strength is now taken as the standard with which other antiseptics are compared.

STUDY QUESTIONS

1. Explain the meaning of Epidemiology.
2. What do you mean by Immunity?

■■■

INDEX

■■■